Quick-and-Easy
STRIP QUILTING

by Helen Whitson Rose

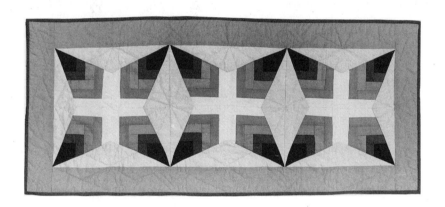

DOVER PUBLICATIONS, INC., New York

Dedicated in love to my family,
Janice, Robin, Ashley, Ray,
Talmadge and Leslie.

The author acknowledges with great appreciation The House of White Birches, Berne, Indiana, and its editors, Sandra L. Hatch and Ruth M. Swasey, for permission to use the following designs and articles that have appeared in their publications. *Stitch 'n Sew Quilts:* "McDougall String Quilt," June 1984; "Economy or Windmill," December 1984; "Mitered Bias Binding," February 1986; "Rocky Road to Kansas Log Cabin," February 1987. *Quilt World:* "Hidden Seam Borders," October 1981; "Estimating Fabrics for Strip Designs," August 1984. *Quilt World Omnibook:* "Estimating Fabric Requirements for Template Shapes," Spring 1982. *Old Homestead Quilt Designs:* "Little House Wall Quilt," 1984 special issue of *Quilt World. Quilt World Christmas Annual:* "Rectangular Courthouse Steps," 1983; "Prosperity Quilt," 1983.

Published in Canada by General Publishing Company, Ltd.,
30 Lesmill Road, Don Mills, Toronto, Ontario.
Published in the United Kingdom by Constable and Company, Ltd.,
10 Orange Street, London WC2H 7EG.

Quick-and-Easy Strip Quilting is a new work,
first published by Dover Publications, Inc., in 1989.

Manufactured in the United States of America
Dover Publications, Inc., 31 East 2nd Street, Mineola, N.Y. 11501

Library of Congress Cataloging-in-Publication Data

Rose, Helen Whitson, 1917–
Quick-and-easy strip quilting / by Helen Whitson Rose.
p.   cm. — (Dover needlework series)
Includes bibliographical references.
ISBN 0-486-26018-6
1. Machine quilting—Patterns. 2. Patchwork—Patterns. I. Title. II. Series.
TT835.R665   1989
738′.092—dc20   89-37989
[B]   CIP

Contents

Introduction

NOT ALL OF US ARE BLESSED WITH AN ABUNDANCE OF TIME FOR quiltmaking, yet we may yearn to make pretty quilts and to play with color and design to soothe that inner craving for creativity. Strip and string quilting techniques enable us to satisfy that craving in a fraction of the time required for more traditional piecing methods.

The use of the sewing machine for piecing strip and string designs is a great time saver in itself. For quick and accurate cutting of strips there is that wonderful tool, the rotary cutter, which rolls across the folded fabric, reducing cutting time and eliminating tedious piece cutting. Although machine piecing is faster, and many strip designs are actually better constructed using the sewing machine, many of the designs can also be sewn by hand if you prefer.

There are five methods for piecing strips to create designs. The simplest method is making strip-pieced material from which shapes and bands are cut that can be used for appliqués, trims and borders. A second method is sewing strips or strings to a shaped base of paper or fabric to create portions of a block design. Another method is sewing combinations of strips together from which squares and triangles are cut and rearranged to form block designs. Then there are the many, many variations of the Log Cabin—strips sewn in sequence around a central shape. The last method, called "quilt-as-you-go," consists of attaching the strips, batting and lining fabric all at the same time. You will find three very different ways for making quilts by this method. Each of these methods will be explained later at length.

I would suggest, if you are not familiar with strip-piecing, that you begin with a small project such as a single block for a pillow, placemat or the front of a tote bag, or three or four blocks for a table runner or small wall hanging. When you have discovered how quickly you can complete one of these projects, you will certainly want to explore other designs for a larger one. Some of the designs allow you to make a choice of methods, and to decide whether to sew by hand or machine. Your choice of colors and placement of light and dark fabrics within the block give you the opportunity to create and explore on your own. Let the ideas in this book stimulate you to change and combine them, so you become your own designer.

The ideas in this book are a continuation of those in my first book, *Quilting with Strips and Strings* (Dover 0-486-24357-5). Much new material has been added, together with all new designs, including many originals.

The material has been organized into chapters according to the different methods. At the beginning of each chapter you will find instructions for the method, followed by several patterns. Each pattern has explicit instructions for quick cutting and sewing, and, in most cases, yardages for making a bed-size quilt. Besides quilts, there are ideas for wall hangings, a pillow, a vest and blocks that can be used a number of different ways. Some designs are simple and easy, while others are more challenging, but all will give you a broad perspective of creating with strips and strings.

I.

General Information

The Rotary Cutter and How to Use It

If you have not purchased a rotary cutting tool, with its special cutting mat and a heavy marked ruler or Plexiglas cutting guides in several widths, do so now, for you will find many uses for this equipment. Use the rotary cutter for all strip-pieced designs, for cutting border strips, for trimming selvages, for cutting bias binding and for cutting small template shapes from strips (read the section "Quick Cuts from Strips", page 6, to discover a time-saving hint for making traditional designs). The time saved in cutting will simply amaze you.

I prefer the heavy-duty rotary cutter that has a circular blade measuring 1¾" across. Replacement blades can also be purchased. To protect the cutting edge of the blade, which is very sharp and can cut from five to eight layers of cotton fabric at a time, and also to protect the worktable, you will need to purchase a cutting mat. These mats, which are of a composition similar to linoleum, come in many sizes. Some are small and portable, while others are much larger and cover most of the work surface. An average size is 12" × 18".

For cutting strips to an exact width, heavy-duty plastic rulers are available. One is the Salem Ruler, 6" × 24" with markings plus a 45° diagonal line. It will cut strips up to 6" wide. Quickline by Nancy Crow, of heavy-duty clear acrylic,

measures 3" × 22½" and is designed to fit across folded 45" wide fabric. It has 12 measurements and will cut strips up to 3" wide. Also available are heavy-duty strip templates of see-through acrylic. A set of five strippers—1½", 2", 2½", 3" and 3½"—is priced about $15.00. I have found that the strip templates I use most often are the 1½" and 2" widths. On the back of my guides, I have glued a 1"-wide strip of fine-grade sandpaper the full length of the guide. This grips the fabric and prevents the guides from slipping as I cut.

Place the cutting mat vertically on the table in front of you. The first cut you make will be to trim the fabric end if it has been torn at the shop, or after you have aligned the grain of the fabric. Start with the fabric folded in half lengthwise as it comes from the bolt, then fold it in half lengthwise one more time. It is now four layers thick and measures about 11" wide (for 45"-wide fabric). Pinning may be necessary to hold the aligned grain of the layers. If

Fig. 1. *The rotary cutter.*

1

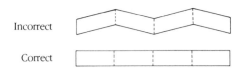

Incorrect

Correct

Fig. 2. *The strips should be perfectly straight, with no points at the folds.*

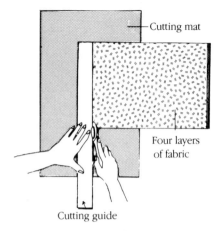

Cutting mat

Four layers of fabric

Cutting guide

Fig. 3. *Place the bulk of the fabric to the right of the cutting mat. Align the cutting guide with the left edge of the fabric.*

you are right-handed, lay the bulk of the fabric to the *left* of the cutting mat. Align the end of the cutting guide farthest away from you with the folded edge of the fabric or with the selvages. Hold the guide down firmly with the left hand and place the blade of the rotary cutter against the guide with the screw head of the cutter to the right. Move the rotary cutter away from you, pressing it firmly against the fabric. Some people prefer to pull the rotary cutter toward them across the fabric; experiment and use the way that is comfortable for you.

Unfold the fabric to examine the first cut. If little points occur at each fold, then the plastic guide was not aligned correctly or the fabric folds need some adjusting. Strive to have absolutely straight strips cut on the straight grain of the fabric *(Fig. 2)*.

Now you are ready to cut the strips for your project. For the second cut, the bulk of the folded fabric should be placed to the *right* of the cutting mat. If you are using a ruler with many markings, it is a good idea to place a piece of tape at the width you will be using. Place the guide over the fabric with the marking at the cut edges and the far end of the guide perpendicular to the fold or selvages. Hold the guide down firmly with the left hand while running the rotary cutter blade close to the guide *(Fig. 3)*. Open out the first strip to check for points along the edges. Now is the time to adjust the fabric and grain before continuing.

Cutting Strips of Odd Widths

Many times you will have to cut strips in an odd width for which there is no acrylic cutting guide or marking on your wide ruler. On a contrasting fabric like muslin or a dark solid, carefully measure with a ruler and cut one strip the desired width. This fabric cutting guide will adhere to the fabric to be cut, and make cutting the strips easy and accurate. Align the fabric cutting guide as you would the plastic guide, place any size acrylic guide over the edge to be cut, and move the rotary cutter along the edge of the acrylic guide. Make sure you are not trimming threads away from your fabric guide as you cut, or your strips will become too narrow. This cutting method is especially useful for printed and dark cottons. For solid fabrics, you can measure the strip width each time with a ruler and mark it several places across the fabric as a guide for placing the acrylic guide. These alternate measuring and cutting methods are also useful if you have purchased limited supplies for the rotary cutter. You should purchase the best marking, cutting and sewing equipment you can afford, for these insure that your project will go successfully from the

beginning without mishaps and delays. Take good care of your equipment and keep moisture away from cutting blades and scissors. A soft eyeglasses case makes a wonderful holder for the rotary cutter.

Fabrics for Strip-Piecing

For many of the strip designs in this book you will be purchasing color-coordinated fabrics that will be cut into strips of a predetermined width. The string designs will utilize irregular lengths and widths from your scrapbag. A quilt design can be coordinated by having certain pieces in each block the same fabric. For these pieces you will probably purchase harmonizing fabrics. Study each design to determine if you want harmonizing colors and fabrics or a scrapbag project. A scrap quilt has great charm because it speaks of usefulness as well as beauty.

There is nothing to equal the ease and pleasure of working with all-cotton fabrics. Fabrics of cotton-and-polyester blends seem to fray more easily and to slip and slide in handling, so try to choose 100% cottons for your quilt projects. Toss the fabric into the washer the day you purchase it, washing light colors together and separately from dark colors. Use the dryer, then press if necessary. One quilter has come up with a great idea for distinguishing washed fabrics from unwashed fabrics in her workroom; she simply makes a small diagonal cut in the selvage at the ends of the washed fabrics! Another way would be to trim the selvages from washed fabrics before you store them.

Quality fabrics are usually woven and pressed with a straight crosswise grain, but often the fabric has been pulled off-grain by the time you purchase it. If you ask the store clerk to tear your cotton fabric from the bolt, you will be able to see how off-grain the fabric is. To straighten the fabric grain, unfold the fabric and sponge it lightly with a damp cloth. Have a friend help you pull the fabric on the bias in many places up and down the selvages until it is straight. It may be necessary to press the fabric on the bias to coax it into alignment so that the selvages meet and the torn ends match straight across. Pin the selvages and ends together as you press. If the selvages seem to keep the fabric from becoming flat, remove them; they are always removed before cutting the pieces for a quilt anyway. It is very necessary that the fabric be on the straight of the grain when cutting strips with the rotary cutter, so work with your fabric before you begin cutting. After the fabric has been straightened and the end of the fabric trimmed, pin the layers together about 6″ from the end to be cut. Each time you have completed cutting a number of strips, pin the cut edges of the folded fabric so it will be ready for next time.

Materials for Block Bases

Many of the patterns in this book call for a block base. A thin, inexpensive, washed muslin is ideal and makes a sturdy block once the strips are attached. Do not choose a heavy muslin since this will make quilting difficult.

Another very good base fabric is the thinnest nonwoven interfacing that can be purchased. One inexpensive brand is Trace-A-Pattern, used for pattern making; another is Magic Transfer. These are 36″ wide and are slightly stiff. Thin interfacing is ideal for hand-sewing strip designs to a shaped base if you do not want to use newsprint paper.

Plain newsprint paper is a wonderful addition to your quilting supplies, for it is economical and serves more than one purpose. When used as a backing for strip-pieced blocks, it can be torn away quickly and easily after the block design is assembled. It is also ideal for drawing large patterns. It is interesting to note that at one time the pages of the Sears, Roebuck catalog were used for backing Log Cabin blocks. The catalog was available to many and, when a page was squared, made a good block size. However, you will find that the unglazed newsprint tears away more easily than catalog pages. Old newspapers that have absorbed the ink should not rub off on your fabrics, so stash some away until you are ready to begin your quilt project. Or, if you prefer, plain newsprint pads are available in art supply stores and ends of rolls of plain newsprint paper may be obtained from a newspaper publisher, often for the asking.

Batting

When the quilt is ready to be assembled or when using the quilt-as-you-go method, batting is used between the top and the lining to give warmth and loft to the finished quilt. Batting can be cotton or polyester. I recommend using polyester batting because it is machine-washable, will dry quickly without lumping, and is available in large, pre-cut seamless sheets.

Decide if your project needs a puffy or a flat look, and choose your batting loft accordingly: the felted-type batting (⅛″ thick) is suitable for garments, craft projects and quilt-as-you-go projects; the glazed, loftier batting is ideal for hand quilting and quilt-as-you-go projects; substantial batting (½″ thick or more) is excellent for hand-tied quilts, and gives quite a puffy effect.

Other Supplies for Marking, Cutting and Sewing

The pleasure of quiltmaking begins with having a well-lighted working surface and the proper equipment.

Scissors

Invest in good dressmaking shears that will cut several layers of fabric easily. Guard these carefully so family members will not abuse them. They should be used only for cutting fabrics, as plastic and paper will soon ruin the cutting edge. I sew with many kinds of scissors—dressmaking shears, old scissors for cutting paper and plastic, small needlework scissors for clipping threads and hand sewing. And I keep scissors in several handy places—with my handwork, at the sewing machine and on my desk.

Pins

Be good to yourself and purchase a box of size 28 (1¾″) extra-long, extra-fine ball-topped pins. These cost about $3.50 for a box of 250, but you will not be buying them every month, for when one drops, it can be easily seen and retrieved. They will easily penetrate several layers of fabric and are a joy to use.

Needles

Quilting needles, called betweens, are available in packages of size 7, 8, 9, 10, 11 and 12. These needles are shorter than other needles, but you will find that the short needle aids in making short stitches. Beginning quilters usually start with a #8 between. When you have graduated to a #10, or even a #12, you are really an accomplished quilter. I use betweens for hand piecing as well as for quilting. Sharps can also be used for hand piecing and come in a variety of sizes. Choose a sharp that is keen and long for better penetration of the fabric.

Thimble

For quiltmaking, you must learn to use a thimble to save your fingers and to help you push the needle through the layers of fabric. Select a thimble for the middle finger of your sewing hand that feels comfortable and is not too tight. The thimble should come almost to the first finger joint and should be flat on the top with grooves or ridges to help you push against the needle. There are now many types of thimbles made to wear on the index finger of the hand under the quilt. One is a leather sheath that is soft enough for you to feel the point of the needle after it penetrates the three layers of a quilt; others are made of plastic or metal. Some quilters put several coats of clear fingernail polish on their index finger to protect it. With so many stitches in a quilt, you will be compelled, sooner or later, to seek a thimble that fits well.

Thread

For machine sewing of strips, hand piecing and appliqué, choose a cotton-wrapped polyester thread for durability. The cotton on the outside keeps static from building up and causing the thread to knot. I also use this thread for quilting, rather than the heavier quilting thread. For machine sewing, choose a neutral color that will blend in with all of the fabric colors. For hand piecing, use a color that matches the darker of the two patches. For appliqué, the thread colors should match the appliqué patches. You may prefer to quilt with off-white thread or you can choose colored thread that complements your work. A matching thread will make your quilting stitches less obvious.

If the thread is causing you problems in hand sewing, run it over a cake of beeswax or a white candle so that it will glide smoothly through the fabric.

Marking Tools

Many strip-pieced designs require marking and cutting across combinations of strips to form squares and triangles, so marking tools are essential. My favorite is the Berol Prismacolor Silver Pencil #949, which is available in stationery stores. The marking appears gray and can be used for marking light or dark fabrics. It can also be used for marking quilting designs. A water-erasable pen is good for marking lines on light-colored fabrics. Simply wipe away the marking with a damp cloth when you have finished quilting. Be sure the marking is completely washed out before using an iron on the fabric, or you might have brown stains. A #3 or #4 hard lead pencil can be used to make a very light line for marking quilting designs. The hardness of the lead will keep the lines from smearing. Never use a dark line or a soft lead pencil when marking a quilt; the lines are next to impossible to remove, even with several washings. There is now a chalk-filled container that dispenses a very fine line of chalk for neat marking of a quilt.

Measuring Tools

Your quilting supplies should contain a variety of rulers. Besides the acrylic cutting guides and wide rulers made especially for strip cutting, you should also have an accurate 12″ ruler and a 6″ ruler for template making. The Mini Quilters' Rule, a 6″ square of heavy clear lucite, is a great tool for cutting out small pieces from strips with the rotary cutter. You should also have a tape measure for measuring fabric yardage.

All of the supplies mentioned in this chapter are available in quilt shops. If you do not have access to a quilt shop, then you might like to order certain supplies by mail. Mail-order sources advertise regularly in quilt magazines. The advertisements in these magazines offer a wealth of information about new products for quilters that make the job easier and quicker. I do not feel that I have finished reading a quilt magazine until I have read all the ads as well as the articles!

Estimating Fabric Requirements for Strip Designs

Strip-pieced designs are usually constructed with a planned fabric and color scheme, and in most cases, fabrics must be purchased. It is therefore necessary to know how much of each fabric to purchase. Many of the patterns in this book have fabric requirements figured for either a full-size quilt or a suggested smaller project, cutting the fabrics with the rotary cutter. If you want to use the patterns for other projects, or if you design your own blocks, you will have to determine the fabric requirements yourself.

Quilts utilizing scrapbag fabric strips do not require fabric estimates, since usually each block is different. However, if the block design has a shaped piece in a fabric that is repeated in all blocks, you may need to estimate the fabric needed for this. See "Estimating Fabric Requirements for Template Shapes" (page 5).

Estimating fabric yardage for strip-pieced designs is not a difficult procedure, but it does require analyzing the block design and the size quilt you wish to make before starting. The following worksheet will carry you through the steps for estimating fabric requirements for any strip design in any size you choose.

It is never a bad idea to make generous estimates so as to allow for straightening the fabric, for any mistakes and for making a sample block. It will help a great deal to jot down all the measurements for your planned design, using the list below. Check your pattern to find some of the figures.

1. Size of finished block (from pattern): ___″ × ___″.
2. Number of blocks in quilt (number of blocks across times number of blocks down): ___″ × ___″.
3. Size of quilt before borders (size of block times number of blocks across, and size of block times number of blocks down): ___″ × ___″.
4. Width of chosen fabric (36″, 42″, 45″, 60″—44″ was used in the following example): ___″.
5. Cut width of strips in the design (be sure to include ¼″ on each side of strip for seam allowances): ___″.
6. Are some strips wider than others in the design? If so, repeat Step 5 for each width strip.
7. Draw a sketch of your block and number the strips (see *Fig. 4*). Now jot down the facts about each strip, following the example and chart in *Fig. 5*. Be sure to include ½″ total seam allowance in the *width* and 2″ extra in the *length* for each strip.
8. Find the total number of running inches of each fabric in one block by adding together the lengths of all the same width strips of that fabric. Multiply by the number of blocks in the quilt; round this figure up to the nearest inch. A total of 45 blocks is used in the example. If you are making a four-block or nine-block wall hanging, then multiply the total inches of one fabric in one block by either four or nine.

Print fabric—46½″ × 45 blocks = 2093″

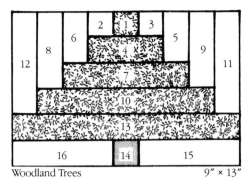

Woodland Trees   9″ × 13″

Fig. 4. Draw a sketch of the block and number the strips.

Blue fabric—62″ × 45 blocks = 2790″
Brown fabric—4″ × 45 blocks = 180″

9. All of the strips are cut across the fabric width, from selvage to selvage, using the rotary cutter, so divide the fabric width (44″ in this case) into the total number of inches to find the number of strips to cut. If any inches are left over in dividing, one more strip should be cut. Place this figure in the chart under "Total Number of Cut Strips."

Print fabric—2093 ÷ 44″ = 47 strips plus 25″. Cut 48 strips.

Blue fabric—2790 ÷ 44″ = 63 strips plus 18″. Cut 64 strips.

Brown fabric—180 ÷ 44″ = 4 strips plus 4″. Cut 4 strips (since so much extra was added in the calculations, a 5th strip will not be needed).

10. For each fabric, multiply the number of strips by the cut width of the strips (2″ in this case).

Print fabric—48 strips × 2″ = 96″ = 2 yds. + 24″. Buy 3 yds.

Blue fabric—64 strips × 2″ = 128″ = 3 yds. + 20″. Buy 3¾ yds.

Brown fabric—4 strips × 2″ = 8″. Buy ⅓ yd.

Put these calculations under "Total Yardage" in chart.

Remember that a little extra fabric is far better than not enough, for fabric cannot always be matched later. Any leftover fabrics can be used for making strip-pieced material as in Method 1.

Estimating Fabric Requirements for Template Shapes

Many times your strip design will have a shaped piece in it to which strips are attached. Here is a simple method to figure yardage for such odd-shaped pieces in a design. See "Traditional Designs in Strips Using Method 1 and Method 2," page 44.

1. Determine the number of blocks in your quilt. As an example we will use *48 blocks*.
2. On the pattern diagram, letter each piece and note your choice of fabric. Also draw the fabric grainline on each piece. The edges of pieces on the outside of the block should be placed on the lengthwise or crosswise grain and as many outside edges as possible of each pattern piece should be on the grain. Also plan grainlines so that you will sew a bias edge on one piece to a straight edge of the adjoining piece.
3. Count the number of identical pieces of each fabric in the pattern. If any pattern pieces are to be reversed to cut some pieces, make a note of it now. This must be taken into consideration when placing pattern pieces as directed below. As an example, we will use *four pieces per block.*
4. Make a paper template of each piece in the pattern, *including the seam allowance.* Mark the fabric and the fabric grainline on each piece.

Fig. 5. *Strip color and size plan for one Woodland Trees block.*

Strip Number	Color	Cut Width of Strip	Length of Strip	Total Number of Cut Strips	Total Yardage
1	Print	2″	2″	Print—48 strips	3 yds.
2	Blue	2″	2″	Blue—64 strips	3¾ yds.
3	Blue	2″	2″	Brown—4 strips	⅓ yd.
4	Print	2″	4½″ + 2″ = 6½″		
5	Blue	2″	3½″ + 2″ = 5½″		
6	Blue	2″	3½″ + 2″ = 5½″		
7	Print	2″	7½″ + 2″ = 9½″		
8	Blue	2″	4½″ + 2″ = 6½″		
9	Blue	2″	4½″ + 2″ = 6½″		
10	Print	2″	10½″ + 2″ = 12½″		
11	Blue	2″	6½″ + 2″ = 8½″		
12	Blue	2″	6½″ + 2″ = 8½″		
13	Print	2″	14″ + 2″ = 16½″		
14	Brown	2″	2″ + 2″ = 4″		
15	Blue	2″	6½″ + 2″ = 8½″		
16	Blue	2″	6½″ + 2″ = 8½″		

Fig. 6. *Fractions of a yard in inches.*

⅛ yd. =	4½″
¼ yd. =	9″
⅓ yd. =	12″
⅜ yd. =	13½″
½ yd. =	18″
⅝ yd. =	22½″
⅔ yd. =	24″
¾ yd. =	27″
⅞ yd. =	31½″
1 yd. =	36″

5. On a length of any kind of fabric, measure and mark with chalk ¼ yard (9″) across the width of the fabric. This could also be done on a large piece of paper measuring 9″ × 44″.

6. Now place one pattern piece on this ¼ yard to determine how many pieces can be cut from this amount of fabric. Be sure to place the pattern on the correct grainline each time. Do not place it over the selvages. Pattern pieces with straight edges may be placed touching so that one cut will separate two pieces, but be sure that seam allowances have been added before doing this. Do not skimp on fabric when placing the pattern pieces. When the calculations have been made, you may want to add a little more for making a sample block and for shrinkage. You should have washed and ironed all fabrics before beginning your quilt to prevent bleeding of colors and shrinkage.

7. Count the number of pieces that fit on the ¼ yard of fabric. As an example we will use *18*.

8. Multiply by four to get the number of pieces that can be cut from one yard. Example: 4 × 18 = 72 pieces from one yard.

9. Multiply the number of blocks in the quilt top by the number of pieces per block.

    Example:

$$\begin{array}{r} 48 \text{ blocks in quilt top} \\ \times\ 4 \text{ pieces in each block} \\ \hline 192 \text{ pieces in quilt top} \end{array}$$

10. Divide the number of pieces cut from one yard (Step 8) into the total number of pieces required for the quilt top (Step 9) to get the total yardage to purchase for that pattern piece.

    Example:

$$\begin{array}{r} 2 \text{ yards} \\ 72\overline{\smash{)}192} \\ \underline{-144} \\ 48 \text{ pieces remaining to be cut} \end{array}$$

Add one more yard of fabric, making the total yardage 3 yards, which will include extra for any mistake, a sample block or waste.

11. Repeat with each pattern piece and fabric used in the quilt top. If more than one piece is cut from the same fabric, the yardages should be added together for the total amount. For pattern pieces that are nearly the same size, you can reuse the calculations for one in order to save time.

12. If one of the fabrics used in the block is also used for the borders, additional yardage of that fabric must be purchased. Decide if you want pieced border strips, or borders cut full length without piecing.

    For pieced borders that are cut across the fabric width, add together the lengths of all four border strips (including the seam allowances), then divide by the fabric width to determine the number of strips to cut. Multiply this by the width of the border strips

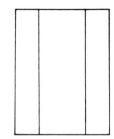

Fig. 7. *For the lining, sew a narrow length to each side of the wider piece.*

(including the seam allowances). You must purchase this much additional fabric.

For unpieced borders, you must purchase a length of fabric that measures at least a little more than the longest border (usually the side border). You may also need additional fabric for pattern pieces. To figure exactly how much fabric you will need, subtract the width of the four border strips from the fabric width. Using the resulting figure as the width of the fabric in Step 5 above, determine how many pieces you can cut from the remaining fabric. Then, if necessary, figure how much additional fabric you will need.

13. The best time to estimate the amount of lining fabric is after the quilt blocks have been sewn together. Measure the length and width of the pieced top and add two inches on *each side* for fastening the lining in the quilt frame. Usually two lengths of 44″-wide fabric are sufficient, unless the quilt top is king-size. Plan your measurements so you will use a full width of fabric down the middle of the lining, with a narrower length sewn to each side *(Fig. 7)*. Always remove the selvages from the lining fabric to prevent puckering of seams, and press the seams to one side, as in block construction.

Quick Cuts from Strips: Cutting Template Shapes from Strips Using the Rotary Cutter

One dreaded job in quiltmaking, especially in traditional patterns using squares, rectangles, triangles, diamonds, parallelograms, etc., is the tedious and time-consuming cutting of many small pieces using templates. Here is a great time saver for cutting a large number of identical pieces for traditional quilt designs, as well as for cutting geometric shapes in strip designs. The secret is using the trusty rotary cutter to cut fabric strips from which template shapes are then cut, meaning that only two sides, usually, of the shape remain to be cut. These methods will also save fabric and enable you to easily calculate fabric yardage.

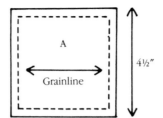

Fig. 8. *Make a template from cardboard or plastic.*

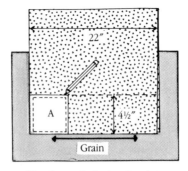

Fig. 9. *Mark the height of the template across the fabric.*

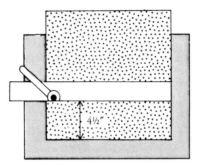

Fig. 10. *Cut the first strip, using the rotary cutter and the acrylic cutting guide.*

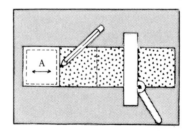

Fig. 11. *Place the template on the strip and mark the cutting lines. Cut the pieces with the rotary cutter.*

1. Make a stiff template of the desired piece, *adding ¼″ seam allowance on all sides.* Mark the pattern piece letter and the fabric grainline on the template *(Fig. 8).*
2. Place the fabric (folded in half lengthwise as it comes from the bolt) on the cutting mat used with the rotary cutter. One end of the fabric should be trimmed with the straight of the fabric grain (see page 1).
3. Position the template on the cut edge of the fabric following the grainline, then measure and mark the height of the template in several places across the fabric *(Fig. 9).*
4. After you have determined the number of template shapes you can cut across the fabric width, calculate the total number of strips necessary for your entire project by dividing the number cut from one strip into the total number required. Multiply the width of one strip (the height of the template) by the number of strips required to get the total inches of fabric to purchase. Divide by 36″ to get the number of yards. Always purchase a little more fabric than is actually needed.
5. Position the acrylic cutting guide on the marks across the folded fabric and cut one strip *(Fig. 10).* Lay this first strip on the fabric again as a guide, position the acrylic cutting guide on the edge to be cut, and cut subsequent strips with the rotary cutter, taking care not to trim threads from the top guide strip.
6. Open out one strip. Position the stiff template on the strip and draw the cutting lines with a ruler and pencil against the stiff template *(Fig. 11).* Straight sides of templates may touch, so that one cut will separate two pieces.
7. Carefully stack two to six strips together with the *marked strip* on top, matching edges and pinning in several places.
8. Position the acrylic cutting guide or the small 6″ Mini Quilters' Rule on the marked lines and cut through all layers with the rotary cutter.

For templates that have curves or many sides like the hexagon, I prefer to use sharp shears for more accurate cutting, but several stacked layers of strips may be cut at one time.

When cutting shapes from strip-pieced material that has many seams in it, make sure it has been pressed on both sides to remove any tucks, and cut *only one layer at a time.*

The presser foot on many sewing machines measures ¼″ from the needle to the edge and can be used as a seam gauge for sewing these cut shapes. Alternatively, you can place a piece of tape on the bed of the machine, so that the edge is ¼″ from the needle. For hand sewing, you may want to draw the sewing line on each piece. An easy way to do this is to make a second stiff template of the shape without the seam allowance, center it on the cut shape, and trace around it with a pencil. If you are an experienced seamstress and can gauge the ¼″ seam allowance by eye, make a dot where the sewing lines cross, or ¼″ in from the edges of the fabric, and sew from dot to dot, leaving the seam allowance free for joining other pieces.

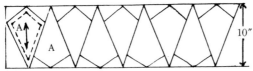

Piece A for String Mountain Star.

Piece #1 for McDougall String Quilt.

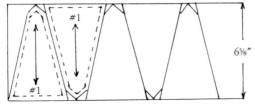

Piece #1 for Star Magic. Cut the long lines with the rotary cutter and the short ends with scissors.

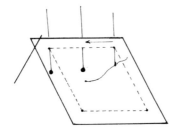

Piece B for Log Cabin Rocky Road to Kansas.

Diamond bases for Stars in Stripes.

Fig. 12. *Marking and cutting various shapes from strips.*

Fig. 13. *Sew from dot to dot, leaving the edges free to join other pieces.*

It is necessary to sew diamonds by the dot-to-dot method in order to leave a ¼″ seam allowance for setting in corner squares and triangles *(Fig. 13)*. If you find you are having problems making the center where many seams come together lie flat, even after pressing all seams to one side and fanning out the center seam allowance, try this solution.

After the seams are pinned together from dot to dot, sew the first half of the seam on the marked seamline; on the rest of the seam (toward the end that will be at the center of the block), sew just *inside* the marked line, just a thread or so, for a wider seam. This small amount of take-up on all seams will make the block flatten out.

Planning a Quilt

The quilt sizes given in this book are a good guide to deciding what size your quilt should be. However, perhaps you like a design, but the size given is not the measurements you need. For instance, you may want to enlarge a design to make a king-size quilt. Perhaps you want a smaller "sleep quilt" with not so much hanging off the sides and extra length at the bottom to tuck under. Or you plan to use the quilt as a bedspread and want it to hang off the sides and bottom with a 12″ allowance included in the length to tuck under a pillow. Maybe you want a square quilt that hangs off the sides and bottom and comes just to the top of the bed so you can use pillow shams. After you have decided which style you like best, the next step is to check the block size in the pattern.

Now you are ready to take tape measure in hand and measure the mattress and height of the bed on which the quilt will be used. A good way to determine what you want is to draw the quilt plan to scale on graph paper, along with notations of the block size and border widths. How many blocks fit across the bed? How many blocks fit into the length you need? Can some blocks be omitted and the quilt enlarged with one, two or three borders? Make sure your design is balanced, usually with an odd number of blocks across and down to fit into your measurements.

Unlike many traditional patchwork patterns, most strip and string designs are set together without strips between the blocks, so that secondary designs are formed. Enlarging a strip quilt with sashing strips is therefore not a good idea. The best way to enlarge the quilt is by making additional blocks or by adding borders.

Another idea is to set the blocks diagonally. The diagonal measurement of a block is greater than the side measurement, so when blocks are set "on point," the measurements increase. Triangular fill-ins are then needed around the sides and ends to make straight sides. Further enlargement can be done by adding or widening the borders *(Fig. 14)*.

Count the number of blocks in your design, then adjust the yardage amounts accordingly.

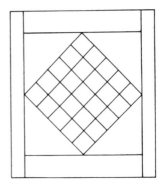

Fig. 14. *Blocks set diagonally with corner triangles and wide borders added to increase the size of the quilt.*

All the steps to quiltmaking are fully covered in *How to Make a Quilt: 25 Easy Lessons for Beginners* by Bonnie Leman and Louise O. Townsend, an excellent guide that should be in every quilter's library.

Borders

A border acts as a frame for the design and is also an excellent way to increase the size of a quilt. The width of the border should be in proportion to the overall size of the quilt. If the quilt is small, then make the border narrow. For bed-size quilts, borders can measure from 2″ to 12″. Borders can have butted ends *(Fig. 15),* corner squares *(Fig. 16)* or mitered corners *(Fig. 17).* On a large quilt, multiple borders can add a nice finishing touch. The work can be accented by a very narrow dark border next to the blocks, then other colored strips or pieced borders can be attached, increasing the quilt size.

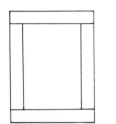 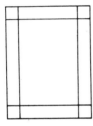 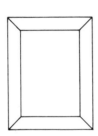

Fig. 15. *Border with butted ends.*   Fig. 16. *Border with corner squares.*   Fig. 17. *Border with mitered corners.*

Measuring and Attaching Borders

The corners of the quilt must be squared and hang properly, and borders must be attached so that ripples do not occur. Therefore careful measurements must be taken. Of course, if you have used accurate seam allowances and measured carefully throughout the construction of the quilt top, then only small adjustments will have to be made. Careful attention to seam allowances and comparing one block to another are required for accuracy.

Measure one side of the quilt top against the opposite side and note this measurement. If one side is shorter than the other, the corners cannot be squared at right angles. Next, measure the top across the center and compare the three measurements. If there is any difference, then adjustments must be made in the block seams until the sides are the same measurement as the center. By taking up several block seams slightly, extra fullness can be eliminated. Do the same for the top in the other direction.

If your border is to have butted ends, decide which borders will be sewn on first—usually the sides. In *Fig. 15,* each side border will measure the length of the side edge plus 2″ for take-up in sewing (the border will be trimmed

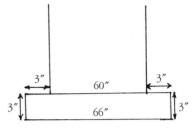

Fig. 18. *Determining the length of the border strip.*

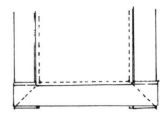

Fig. 19. *Marking the mitered corners.*

after attaching it), by the desired width of the border plus ½″ for seam allowances. The top and bottom borders will each measure the length of the top or bottom edge plus twice the width of the side border plus 2″ for take-up, by the desired width plus ½″.

For a border with corner squares, each border strip should measure the length of the edge to which it is to be attached, by the desired width plus ½″. Each side of the corner square should be equal to the cut width of the border. Sew the side borders to the quilt. Sew a corner square to each end of the top and bottom borders, then sew these strips to the quilt, carefully matching the seams.

For a border with mitered corners, measure the edge of the quilt top and the width of the border. Add the width of the border to both ends of the edge measurement *(Fig. 18).* Attach the border to one edge of the quilt top, starting and stopping ¼″ in from the edge of the quilt top, leaving a seam allowance to attach the other borders. Attach the remaining borders in the same way. On the wrong side of each end of the border, draw a line at a 45° angle from the end of the seam to the outside edge of the border. Pin the marked lines together on the wrong side. Lay the corner on a flat surface and check to see that the border is flat and the corner is square. Baste, then machine-stitch on the marked lines *(Fig. 19).*

Hidden Seam Borders

Here is an ingenious method for attaching a border to a quilt made by the quilt-as-you-go method, or for repairing frayed edges on an old quilt. Any quilt that has already been quilted can have a padded border added at a late hour by this butted-end method, and no one will ever know that the border was an afterthought.

For the border, choose one of the fabrics used in the quilt top, or a harmonizing print or solid fabric. You will also need a lining strip for each border. Use the same fabric to save buying more fabric, or match the lining of the quilt. A total of eight border strips are required—four side lengths, and four end lengths.

Refer to page 9 to prepare the quilt edges. Measure the quilt lengthwise and add 6″ for take-up in sewing and for squaring-off the border ends. Purchase this amount of fabric for cutting lengthwise border strips. If the borders are to be pieced, less fabric is required.

Decide on the width of the border, making it in proportion to the rest of the quilt. Borders of several colors may be added by this method, attaching the borders to all four sides of the quilt before adding another color. Four lengthwise borders as wide as 11″ can be cut across a 45″ fabric width, but usually the borders will not be this wide. Any leftover fabric can be turned into ruffles to use on matching pillow shams, or in another quilt project.

Purchase batting similar to the batting in the quilt. The batting strips are cut the same width and length as the border strips. Shorter strips of batting may be joined by whip-stitching the ends together, then gently pulling the seam so the edges of the batting just butt together.

Cutting and Assembling the Border "Sandwich"

1. Measure the length of the quilt and add 6″ for take-up in sewing and for squaring off the ends.
2. Decide on the border width.
3. The border strips are attached to the longer sides of the quilt first. Cut two borders the length of the quilt, plus 6″. Cut two border lining strips and two batting strips, all this same length and width.
4. Make a "sandwich" of the border layers and the finished quilt *(Fig. 20)*. The border layers should extend 2″ to 3″ beyond the edges of the quilt. Beginning with the bottom layer "e," stack:
   e. *Border lining*, right side up. The seam will be on the right edge of this strip.
   d. *Completed quilt,* with the edges trimmed straight if necessary, right side up.
   c. *Border,* wrong side up.
   b. *Batting strip.*
Match all the edges evenly on the right edge of the stacked layers and baste the layers together.
   a. 2″-wide paper strip (newspaper is good) placed over the batting to make all the layers feed easily under the presser foot of the sewing machine.

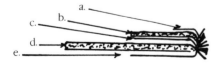

Fig. 20. *Stacking the border layers for stitching.*

5. Stitch the layers, taking up a ¼″ or ⅜″ seam. Keep the bulk of the quilt to the left, resting on the machine table. Adjust the machine pressure for thicker fabrics and use a stitch setting of six to ten stitches per inch. Place your left hand to the left of the machine needle to guide the layers gently under the presser foot and pull the work gently toward the back with the right hand. Remove the paper strip. The border can also be attached by hand, taking small stitches through all layers, and backstitching every few inches.
6. After stitching, turn the border layers to the right side, so that the seam and batting will be inside; baste close to the seam. Using a T-square, triangle or sheet of paper, square off each end of the border at the outside edge, even with the top and bottom edges of the quilt. The corners must be at true right angles at the outside edges.
7. Take the measurement for the top and bottom borders after the side borders are stitched, turned and basted. The measurement will equal the width of the quilt, plus two border widths, plus 6″ extra for take-up in sewing. As an example, if the quilt is 60″ wide, and the border is 3″ wide, the end border will be 66″, plus 6″ extra, for a total of 72″. Cut two borders, two border linings and two batting strips, all the same length and width, for the ends of the quilt. Attach to the ends of the quilt following Steps 4, 5 and 6. After trimming, the ends of these borders will line up with the outside edges of the side borders and must be at right angles at the outside edges for a perfect corner.

Pin and baste the outside edges of the borders. A quilting design can now be marked on the border and hand-quilted, either in the lap or in a small frame or hoop. Add a mitered bias binding to finish the edges of the quilt.

Mitered Bias Binding

This method of finishing the edge of your quilt will score top points with the quilt judges! The ends and edges of quilts seem to take the hardest wear, so a doubled bias binding will last many years longer than merely bringing the folded edge of the quilt top or lining to the other side and stitching it down.

To determine the length of the binding needed, measure the quilt on all four sides. Add 12″ to this measurement for mitering the corners. One yard to 1¼ yards of 45″-wide fabric is usually ample for your bias strips. To find the true bias, fold the fabric on a 45° angle with the straight-cut end touching one selvage; press with the iron. Cut on this fold but do not separate the layers. With a ruler and pencil, mark 2¼″ away from the cut edge and cut strips through the two layers. Pin the edges of the fabric together. Continue to mark and cut strips as needed. I prefer to use scissors for

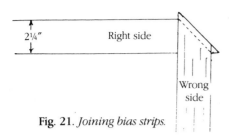

Fig. 21. *Joining bias strips.*

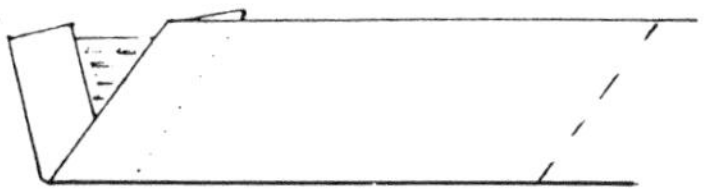

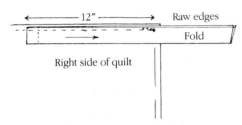

Fig. 22. *Fold the bias strip in half lengthwise.*

Fig. 23. *Sew to the dot at the first corner of the quilt.*

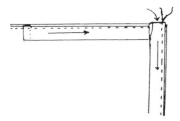

Fig. 25. *Fold the binding down and sew the next side of the quilt.*

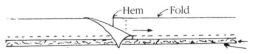

Fig. 26. *Overlap the ends of the binding.*

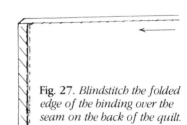

Fig. 24. *Fold the binding straight up, forming a 45° angle.*

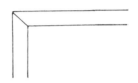

Fig. 27. *Blindstitch the folded edge of the binding over the seam on the back of the quilt.*

Fig. 28. *The corners are automatically mitered on the front of the quilt.*

cutting on the marked lines because of stretching, but you may use the rotary cutter, 2¼″ guide and cutting mat if the equipment does not slip out of place for you.

Now follow these steps for a successful finish to your quilt.

1. Cut bias binding 2¼″ wide. To join the ends of the bias strips, match the diagonal edges by letting the top bias strip extend beyond the bottom strip by at least ⅜″. Begin and end the stitching at the angles *(Fig. 21)*. Press the seam open.

2. Cut one end of the strip straight across and fold under a ½″ hem. Fold the binding in half lengthwise with the right side out; press with the iron *(Fig. 22)*.

3. On the right side of the quilt top, make a dot at each of the four corners, ¼″ in from the edges, where the seams will meet at right angles.

4. Start the binding 6″ to 12″ to the left of one corner of the quilt. Place the raw edges of the folded binding against the raw edges of the quilt on the right side. Working from left to right, machine-stitch a ¼″ seam to the dot. Backstitch and remove the work from the sewing machine. Do not sew to the edge of the quilt at the right *(Fig. 23)*.

5. Fold the binding straight up away from the corner, forming a 45° angle *(Fig. 24)*.

6. Fold the binding straight down with the raw edges matching the next side of the quilt to be sewn, and making a straight fold even with the first sewn edge at the top. Begin stitching the next side of the binding at the top edge *(Fig. 25)*. Continue sewing to the next corner, ending at the dot and backstitching. Make the same fold in the binding at each corner.

7. Overlap the ends of the binding *(Fig. 26)*.

8. Do not trim the seam allowance as this will act as padding in the binding. Turn the binding to the back over the seam. Working from right to left, blindstitch the binding in place *(Fig. 27)*. The front of the binding will automatically have a mitered corner *(Fig. 28)*.

9. To finish the miter on the back side, blindstitch right up to the corner formed by the machine stitching and take a few stitches to secure. Fold the next side over

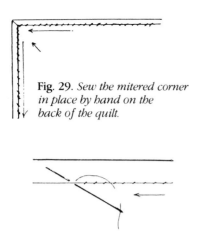

Fig. 29. *Sew the mitered corner in place by hand on the back of the quilt.*

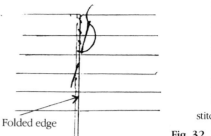

Folded edge

Fig. 31. *Top basting from the right side of the fabric.*

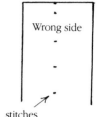

Wrong side

stitches

Fig. 32. *The tiny stitches on the wrong side will be the guideline for stitching the seam.*

Fig. 30. *To blindstitch, bring the needle up from under the binding into the folded edge of the binding. Insert the needle down into the lower fabric and up again into the folded edge of the binding in one motion. Make the stitches very close together.*

the machine stitching, forming a 45° angle from the outside corner to the stitched edge of the binding. Continue sewing the folded edge of the binding, forming neat miters at each corner of the quilt *(Fig. 29).*

Top Basting: A Neat Trick for Matching Cross Seams

With many seams to match when joining strip-pieced blocks together, it may be difficult at times to make the seams match up just by pinning and basting. One of my tricks for matching seams is *top basting,* which is often used to match plaids and checks in dressmaking. The technique is simply an overlapped seam basted from the top side.

Work from top to bottom for basting on the right side of the fabric. Fold under ¼″ or more on the *left* side of the work, then place this over the other layer, matching the cross seams exactly. Pin in several places. Beginning at the top, take a tiny blindstitch, similar to that used in appliqué work, into the folded edge, then insert the needle into the bottom layer just where the thread comes out of the fold and sweep the needle forward about ½″ up into the folded top edge again *(Fig. 31).* Catch only a thread or two on the folded edge each time. The stitches do not have to be close together for basting this way; however, they should be very small on the edge of the fold.

Now fold the two matched pieces with right sides together to see the tiny basted stitches on the wrong side *(Fig. 32).* These will be the guideline for machine or hand stitching. Remove the basting stitches after the seam is completed.

This method is useful for both horizontal and vertical seams. It is also the technique used on the back of quilts assembled by the quilt-as-you-go method. You will find many more places in your sewing and quilting to use this method for matching and joining seams exactly.

Pressing Strip-Pieced Designs

When strips are joined together, it is very important that the work be pressed as it progresses, so that the many seams will flatten out, and puckers or tiny pleats are not formed on the right side.

With the steam setting on the iron, first press each seam flat on the wrong side to "relax" the stitching and fabric. Then press the seam to one side, preferably toward the darker fabric. Do this for each seam in the work. Now turn the work to the right side and press again to remove puckers and tiny pleats near the seams. When shapes such as squares and triangles are cut from combination strips with several seams, it is necessary that the strip fabric be flat and straight for marking and cutting properly. Blocks pieced by other methods must be pressed into a true square. Make a cardboard template the size of the block and press your squares over this.

Suggested Reading

Bonesteel, Georgia. *Lap Quilting with Georgia Bonesteel.* Oxmoor House, 500 Office Park Drive, Birmingham, AL 35225.

Bonesteel, Georgia. *More Lap Quilting with Georgia Bonesteel.* Oxmoor House, 500 Office Park Drive, Birmingham, AL 35225.

Leman, Bonnie, and Martin, Judy. *Log Cabin Quilts.* Moon Over the Mountain Publishing Company, 6700 West 44th Avenue, Wheatridge, CO 80033.

Leman, Bonnie, and Martin, Judy. *Taking the Math Out of Making Patchwork Quilts.* Moon Over the Mountain Publishing Company, 6700 West 44th Avenue, Wheatridge, CO 80033.

Leman, Bonnie, and Townsend, Louise O. *How to Make a Quilt: 25 Easy Lessons for Beginners.* Moon Over the Mountain Publishing Company, 6700 West 44th Avenue, Wheatridge, CO 80033.

Millett, Sandra. *Quilt-As-You-Go.* Chilton Book Company, Chilton Way, Radnor, PA 19089.

Rose, Helen Whitson. *Quilting with Strips and Strings.* Dover Publications, Inc., 31 East 2nd Street, Mineola, NY 11501-3582.

II.

Method 1: Making String or Strip Material

STRING OR STRIP MATERIAL IS A FABRIC COMPOSED OF LONG STRIPS OF material that have been sewn together. It is often pieced from scrapbag fabrics, utilizing long pieces left over from other sewing projects. The fabric strips do not have to be a uniform width. In fact, using strips of different widths will add interest to the finished piece of strip material. Color is an important factor to consider in placing the fabric strips. You can use light next to dark, dull next to bright and print next to solid to create different effects. Generally, using strips with different patterns will create a more interesting fabric than using strips with similar patterns.

The width of your pieced strip material is dictated by the length of the fabric strips used to construct it. Sort your strips into groups of similar lengths before sewing. Sew these groups together to eliminate waste. You will end up with several different widths of strip material, all of which will be usable *(Figs. 33 and 34)*.

To construct your strip material, place the strips right sides in and sew the pieces together in a narrow seam. Set the machine for 12 stitches to the inch. If you are sewing by hand, make very tiny stitches and backstitch about every inch or so. Different effects can be achieved by rotating the fabric strips slightly as you join them, making the strip wider at one end and adding interest to the pieced fabric *(Figs. 35 and 36)*. For a more structured look, use strips cut to the same width and a constant ¼″ seam allowance *(Fig. 37)*.

Sew strips of similar-length fabric together until you have reached the desired size of string material, keeping in mind that the size of the material will increase considerably after pressing. Using the steam iron, press each seam flat on the wrong side as sewn, then press the seams to one side toward the darker fabric if possible. Now turn the fabric over to the right side and press again to remove any pleats or tucks at the seam. Pressing is absolutely necessary to make the fabric flat for cutting shapes.

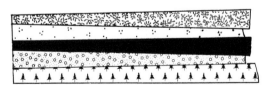

Fig. 33. *Sewing strips of similar lengths together— an efficient way to make strip material.*

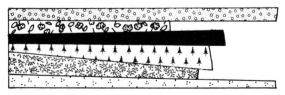

Fig. 34. *Sewing strips of dissimilar lengths together, resulting in a wastage of fabric.*

13

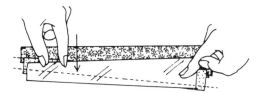

Fig. 35. *Rotating strips slightly before sewing.*

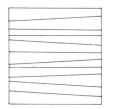 

Fig. 36. *Unstructured strip material.*

Fig. 37. *Structured strip material.*

Fig. 38. *Using strip material to make an appliqué.*

Fig. 39. *Using strip material as a background for appliqué.*

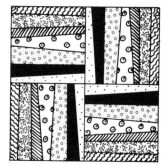

Fig. 40. *Creating a design from blocks of strip material.*

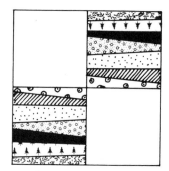

Fig. 41. *Alternating blocks of solid and strip material.*

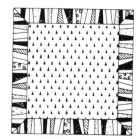

Fig. 42. *Strip-pieced edging.*

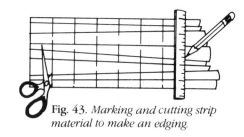

Fig. 43. *Marking and cutting strip material to make an edging.*

Using Strip Material: Strip material can be used in many ways. Use the strip material to cut out appliqué shapes *(Fig. 38)* or as a background fabric for plain appliqué designs *(Fig. 39)*. You can cut the strip material into blocks, then sew the blocks together, alternating the strips vertically and horizontally *(Fig. 40)*, or alternate blocks of strip material with solid blocks *(Fig. 41)*.

An attractive border or edging can be made from strip material *(Fig. 42)*. First construct a wide piece of strip material, then mark the desired width of the edging plus ½″ seam allowance on the material using a ruler and pencil *(Fig. 43)*. Cut the strips along the marked lines and join the pieces end to end for the desired border length. These pieced strips can also be part of a block design, as in Sewing Circle, page 55. A strip edging can add a distinctive finishing touch to a simple quilt or pillow, and can also be used on collars, cuffs, yokes and hems of garments.

See Chapter IV for examples of other ways to use strip material within a block design.

Make sure the template shapes you cut from the strip material have ¼″ seam allowances included, and cut only one layer of strip material at a time for accuracy.

Strip-Pieced Butterfly Pillow

Method: Appliqués cut from strip-pieced material.
Finished Block Size: 15½″ square.
Materials:

½ yd. 45″-wide light-colored solid fabric for pillow front and back.

Eight strips for strip material, cut 1½″ wide across the full width of 45″-wide fabric. Use harmonizing colors and some repeats for a structured look. Strips of random widths may be used for an unstructured look.

Scraps of black fabric for wing spots and body.

½ yd. contrasting fabric for ruffle.

2 yds. narrow lace edging.

½ yd. muslin for inner pillow.

Polyester fiberfill.

Black embroidery floss.

Sewing thread to match fabrics.

Optional: 4 yds. of black piping for wings and spots.

Trace the patterns for the wings, wing spots and body, including the seam allowances. Cut from paper.

Make strip material at least 33″ across by 8″ high. Sew the strips together, using ¼″ seams. Press the seams flat as sewn, then to one side. Press again on the right side. Place the patterns for the upper wing A and the lower wing B on the strip material, having the lines in the patterns parallel to the seams of the strips *(Fig. A)*. Cut out the wings. For the other pair of wings, pin the cut-out wings, *wrong side up,* on the strip material, matching the seams and the colors of the strips. Cut out the reversed wings. Cut two each of upper wing spot C and lower wing spot D and one body E from black. Mark the center lines on the body with basting or by folding and creasing the folds. Turn under and baste a ¼″ hem on all pieces.

Cut a 16″ square of light fabric for the pillow top. Fold in half lengthwise, then crosswise, to mark the horizontal and vertical center. Pin the wings and wing spots to the block, with the wing points toward the center of the block and separated by about ¼″; baste. Blindstitch all edges using matching thread. Pin the body over the wings, matching the center lines of the body and the pillow top; blindstitch in place *(Fig. B)..*

Piping may be added to the edges of the wings before basting them to the pillow top. First, soak the piping in very hot water to shrink the string; allow it to dry thoroughly. Starting at the point of the wing, baste piping around the right side of each wing with the raw edges even. Machine-stitch the piping in place, then turn the raw edges under. Baste the wings in position, and stitch around each wing, stitching "in the ditch" between the wing and the piping.

To accent the work, embroider an even running stitch around all the pieces, using six strands of black embroidery floss. Embroider the antennae in outline stitch using three strands of black floss *(Fig. C)*.

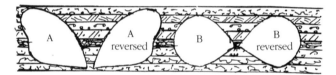

Fig. A. *Cut the wings from strip-pieced material.*

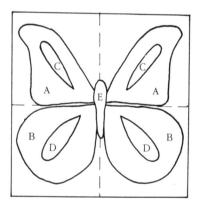

Fig. B. *Blindstitch the wings, wing spots and body to the block.*

For the ruffle, cut three 6″-wide strips across the full width of contrasting fabric. With right sides in, join the short ends of the strips to make a long strip. Baste the narrow lace to the right side of one long edge, matching the raw edges. Join the ends of the ruffle strip to make a circle; press the seams open. With the wrong side in, bring the raw edges of the strip together; press. Divide the ruffle into quarters with pins, being careful that the pins do not fall over the seams. Sew a row of gathering stitches about ½″ from the edge of

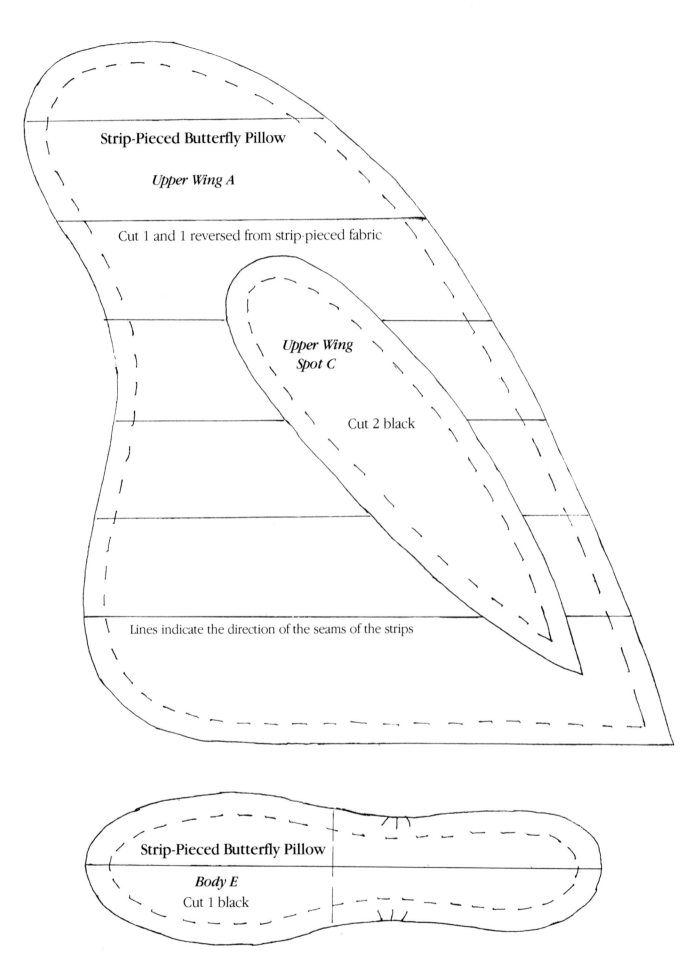

Strip-Pieced Butterfly Pillow

Upper Wing A

Cut 1 and 1 reversed from strip-pieced fabric

Upper Wing Spot C

Cut 2 black

Lines indicate the direction of the seams of the strips

Strip-Pieced Butterfly Pillow

Body E
Cut 1 black

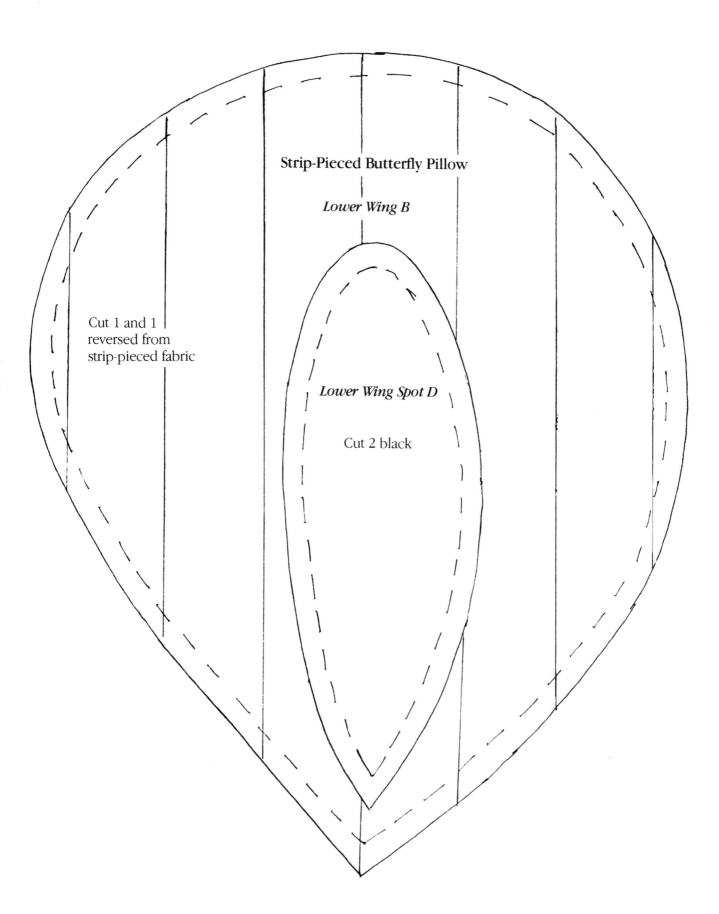

Strip-Pieced Butterfly Pillow

Lower Wing B

Cut 1 and 1
reversed from
strip-pieced fabric

Lower Wing Spot D

Cut 2 black

Fig. C. *Embroider the antennae in outline stitch.*

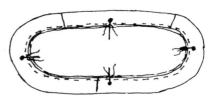

Fig. D. *Sew a row of gathering stitches around the edge of the ruffle.*

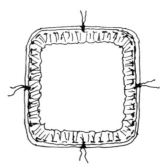

Fig. E. *Gather the ruffle to fit the edges of the pillow top.*

the ruffle, beginning and ending at the pins *(Fig. D)*. Pull up the bobbin thread to gather the ruffle.

Mark the center of each edge of the pillow top. Pin the ruffle to the right side of the pillow top, having the raw edges even and matching the pins to the center of each edge. Make sure that the lace-trimmed side is against the right side of the pillow top. Gather the ruffle to fit the pillow edges, distributing the gathers evenly and having extra fullness at the corners. Baste, then stitch *(Fig. E)*. Cut the pillow back 16″ square. With right sides in and the ruffle between, pin the pillow top and back together. Stitch, leaving an opening on the bottom of the pillow. Turn the pillow right side out.

Cut two 16″ squares of muslin and stitch them together, leaving an opening for turning. Turn this inner pillow right side out and stuff firmly. Slipstitch the opening. Insert the muslin pillow form inside the pillow and slipstitch the opening.

Floating Heart Trim

This trim can be used down the front or around the bottom of vests, jackets or other items. The method is similar to reverse appliqué using strip-pieced fabric underneath. Make a sample before working on your garment.

Make strip-pieced fabric 6″ high and long enough to cut as many 6″ squares as there are hearts on your garment. The strips can vary in cut width from ¾″ to 1½″. Stitch the strips together using ¼″ seams. Press the seams flat as sewn, then to one side; press again on the right side to remove any tucks. To embellish the strips, sew narrow lace or ribbon across the right side of the strips. Soak the lace and ribbon in hot water to shrink them and allow to dry before sewing in place.

Cut 6″ squares from the strip-pieced fabric—one for each heart *(Fig. A)*. For each heart, also cut a 6″ square from the same fabric as the garment to use as a facing for the heart-shaped hole. Trace the heart in *Fig. B* on the solid lines and cut a template from lightweight cardboard or plastic.

Center the heart template on the wrong side of the facing square and trace around it. Mark the placement of the heart on the right side of the garment using a removable chalk pencil.

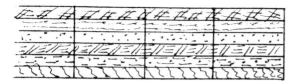

Fig. A. *Cut 6″ squares from strip-pieced material.*

Place the facing square, marked side up, over the marking on the garment, matching the lines carefully; machine-stitch accurately on the marked lines, beginning at one side of the heart and using a stitch length of ten stitches to the inch. At the points of the heart, keep the needle in the fabric and pivot the fabric; continue stitching the next side. Overlap the stitching at the end.

Cut ¼″ inside the machine stitching. Clip into the seam allowance at the bottom point of the heart; trim straight across at the top point, then clip into the seam allowance on the curved edges (see *Fig. B*). Turn the facing to the wrong side of the garment, letting 1/16″ show on the top side. Baste and press.

Place the strip-pieced square under the heart opening with the right side showing through the opening. The seam lines of the strips can be vertical, horizontal or diagonal. Baste the strip-pieced square *to the facing* only. Baste again about ½″ away from the seams of the heart, then fold back the garment so that the facing side of the opening will be on top. Machine-stitch straight lines about ¼″ away from the seams of the heart (see the long broken lines in *Fig. B*). Trim away the excess fabric outside the last machine stitches to reduce bulk. On the right side, the heart will appear to float because the seam cannot be seen. Finish the garment with a lining.

Any small, shaped opening can be constructed in this way. A faced opening of 3″ to 5″ works best. Your choice of strip colors and lace and ribbon embellishments will give an individual touch to this trim.

Fig. B. *Pattern for the heart.*

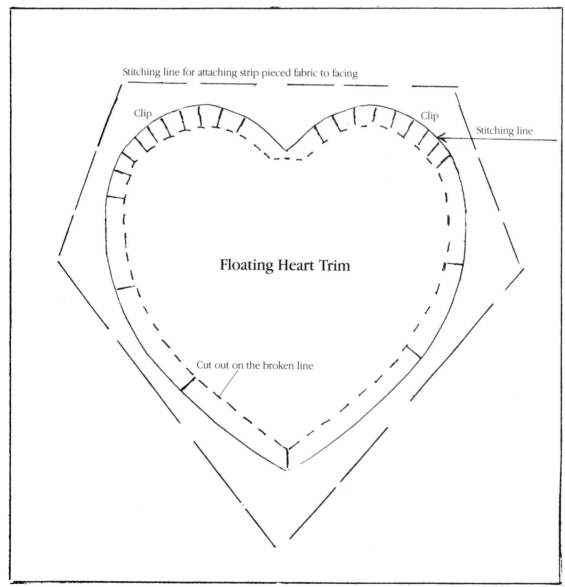

Stitching line for attaching strip-pieced fabric to facing

Clip

Clip

Stitching line

Floating Heart Trim

Cut out on the broken line

String Tulip Appliqué

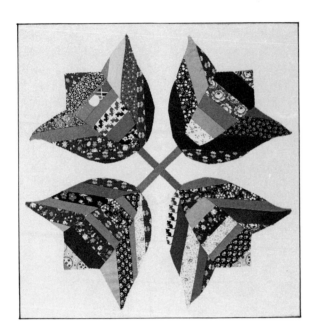

Method 1

Make string material using strips of various widths and colors, keeping the seams of the strips parallel. Placing the arrows on the templates parallel to the seams of the strips, cut 80 of center petal A and 80 of side petal B *(Fig. A)*. Turn Template B over and cut 80 reversed side petals.

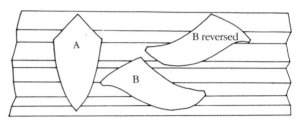

Fig. A. *Cut the petals from strip-pieced material.*

Method 2

From newspaper or thin fabric, cut bases for 80 of center petal A and 160 of side petal B. Half of the B bases will be turned over to reverse the petal. For each petal, pin the first strip across the base, keeping it parallel to the arrow on the pattern *(Fig. B)*. Continue to add strips until the base is covered (see page 22). Trim the excess fabric even with the edges of the base. Tear away paper if used.

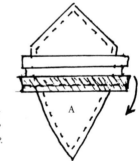

Fig. B.
Sew strips across the petal base.

Method 1: Appliqués cut from string-pieced material.
Method 2: Scrap strings sewn to a shaped base for appliqué pieces (see "Method 2: Strips Assembled on a Shaped Base," page 23).
Finished Block Size: 18″.
Number of Blocks for Quilt: 20.
Setting: Five blocks down by four blocks across; no sashing strips.
Quilt Size: 72″ × 90″ without borders; 80″ × 98″ with a 4″-wide border.
Materials for Quilt:
   5 yds. muslin or other solid color fabric for blocks.
   6 yds. brown or green ½″-wide single-fold bias binding or scraps of green or brown fabric for stems.
   5 yds. fabric for lining.
   Threads to match fabric.
   Newspaper or 2 yds. 36″-wide very thin nonwoven interfacing for bases (Method 2 only).
   For optional borders: 2¾ yds. of fabric.
   Batting.

This lovely old scrap-pieced design is still a favorite. Since this is a scrap quilt, no yardage is given for the string-pieced flowers. When made by Method 2, this design can use the smallest scraps in your scrapbag. Be sure to include the seam allowances when making the templates.

Trace the patterns for the petals, including the seam allowances and cut templates from lightweight cardboard or plastic. Cut twenty blocks, 18½″ square.

Mark the notches and "dots" at the ends of the seams on the wrong side of all the pieces. For each tulip, sew a side petal to each side of a center petal, starting and stopping the seam at the "dot" on the pattern. Turn under a ¼″ hem on the outside edges of the tulip and baste. Make four tulips for each block.

To mark the placement lines for the tulips, fold the block in half diagonally and crease; repeat in the opposite direction. Use bias tape for the stems or cut two 1″ by 4½″ pieces of green or brown fabric. Press under ¼″ on the long edges of the fabric strips. Pin a stem to the block, centering it along one of the diagonal creases. Pin the other stem over the other diagonal crease. The stems should cross at the

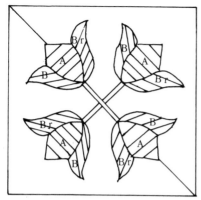

Fig. C. *Blindstitch the pieces to the block.*

center of the block. Place a tulip over each end of each stem, adjusting the tulips so that the centers are on the creases and there is about 3½″ of stem between the flowers. Blindstitch the pieces in place with matching thread *(Fig. C)*.

Sew the blocks together in five rows of four blocks each. Sew the rows together. If desired, cut two side borders 4½″ × 92″ and two end borders 4½″ × 82″. Sew the side borders, then the end borders to the quilt. Place the quilt top over the batting and lining; quilt as desired and bind the edges.

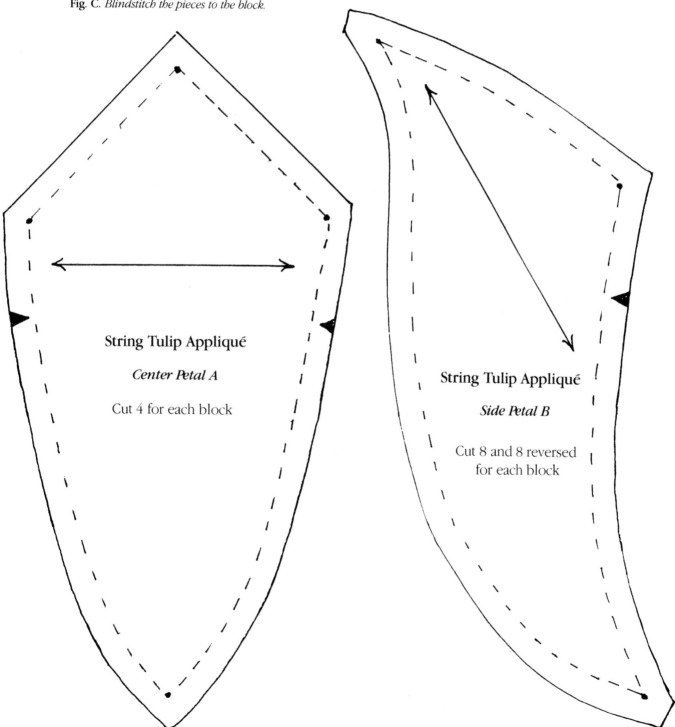

String Tulip Appliqué

Center Petal A

Cut 4 for each block

String Tulip Appliqué

Side Petal B

Cut 8 and 8 reversed
for each block

III.

Method 2: Strips Assembled on a Shaped Base

MANY DESIGNS, OR PARTS OF DESIGNS, CAN BE MADE BY SEWING STRIPS to a shaped base cut from newspaper or thin fabric. For example, String Mountain Star is a very simple design made on a square of newspaper. Using this method, almost any shape—squares, triangles, diamonds, or even odd-shaped curved pieces—can be made of strips, then assembled into a design or block. Many Log Cabin designs are assembled on a base square, and many other traditional designs can incorporate pieces constructed in strips on a shaped base. See "Traditional Designs in Strips Using Method 1 and Method 2," page 44.

For a paper base, use old newspapers (that have absorbed most of the ink so that it will not smear onto the fabric and your hands), or beg the end of a roll of newsprint from a printer. The newspaper tears away easily after the pieces are assembled.

For a fabric base, use lightweight material, such as thin muslin, that is compatible in fiber content with the strips you will be applying to it. Prepare the fabric base by washing and ironing it to preshrink it.

There is a very thin nonwoven interfacing available in the fabric stores called Trace-A-Pattern that makes an excellent base, especially for hand sewing. It does not need washing, does not add unwanted thickness, nor does it make quilting difficult, yet it helps to stabilize the stitching to the shaped base.

The size and shape of the base will depend upon what you are making. Each design in this chapter gives the pattern for the base shape including seam allowances, or gives instructions for marking and cutting the base. The base shape *must include seam allowances* for attaching other pieces of the design.

Cut the base according to the pattern instructions. On the back of the base, mark the outside sewing line ¼″ away from the edge. Place the base right side up on a flat surface, then place the first strip right side up across the base so that the ends extend slightly beyond the base on each side. In this method, strips are not cut to a specific length before sewing, but are trimmed after sewing, leaving about ½″ extending on both sides of the base. Place the second strip over the first with right sides together and pin it along one edge. Before sewing, turn the second strip to the right side to make sure the ends will cover the base. Sew both strips to the base ¼″ from the pinned edge, making sure that the pieces remain flat and smooth as they feed through the sewing machine. Remove the pins. Press the second strip as it is sewn to set the stitches, then turn it to the right side and press again to remove any tucks or pleats. Pin the second strip through the seam to make it flatten out. Continue adding strips to each side of the first strip until the entire base is covered, pressing after the addition of each strip. Turn the work to the wrong side and trim the excess fabric even with the edge of the base. The marked seamlines will be visible on the wrong side of the base fabric. If using a paper base, pull the fabric slightly on the bias in the opposite direction to the rows of stitching to release the paper, then gently tear away the paper without distorting the sewn fabric. Press carefully on both sides to remove tucks and pleats at the seams.

String Mountain Star

Method: Strips sewn to a shaped base.
Finished Block Size: 13″.
Number of Blocks for Quilt: 20.
Setting: Four blocks across by five blocks down. No sashing strips are used, so secondary strip-pieced diamonds are formed where the blocks touch.
Quilt Size: Approximately 52″ × 65″ without borders.
Materials for Quilt

Note: Yardage is calculated for cutting with the rotary cutter. All strips are cut across the full width of the fabric. Do not cut the strips to a specific length before attaching them to the base.

45″-wide fabrics:

1½ yds. green solid for strip #1. Cut 32 strips 1½″ wide.

1¼ yds. red/white/green print for strip #2. Cut 25 strips 1½″ wide.

1 yd. red solid for strip #3. Cut 16 strips 1½″ wide.

2½ yds. white for wedge A. Cut seven strips 10″ wide.

4 yds. for lining.

4 yds. 36″-wide lightweight interfacing for bases. Newspaper may also be used.

Batting.

Trace the patterns for the base and for wedge A, including the seam allowances. Cut templates from lightweight cardboard or plastic. Following *Fig. A,* placing the arrow on the template on the straight grain of the fabric, cut 80 A wedges from the 10″-wide white strips (12 wedges should fit across each strip). Cut 80 bases from interfacing or newspaper. If interfacing is used, the rotary cutter may be used to cut the bases. Do not use the rotary cutter to cut newspaper, as this will dull the blade.

Pin an A wedge diagonally across a base square. Taking a ¼″ seam, sew a #1 strip to each side of the A wedge. Cut the ends of the strip so that they extend about ½″ beyond the edges of the base. Turn the strip to the right side. Press the strip along the seam, then pin it to the base through the seam. Add strip #2, then #3 to each side to cover the square completely *(Fig. B).* Press the square, then trim the strips even with the edges of the base square. Repeat for all squares. If newspaper has been used for the bases, tear it away before joining the squares, being careful not to distort the fabric.

For each block, sew four squares together so that the wide ends of the A wedges meet at the center of the block *(Fig. C).*

Sew the blocks together to form five rows of four blocks each, then sew the rows together. The quilt can be enlarged by adding borders or by making 30 blocks and setting them

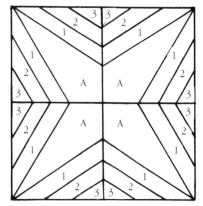

Fig. B. *Adding strips to the base square.*

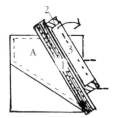

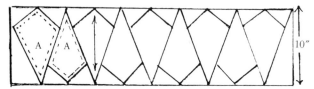

Fig. A. *Trace A wedges to the 10″-wide white strip and cut.*

Fig. C. *Four squares joined to make a block.*

23

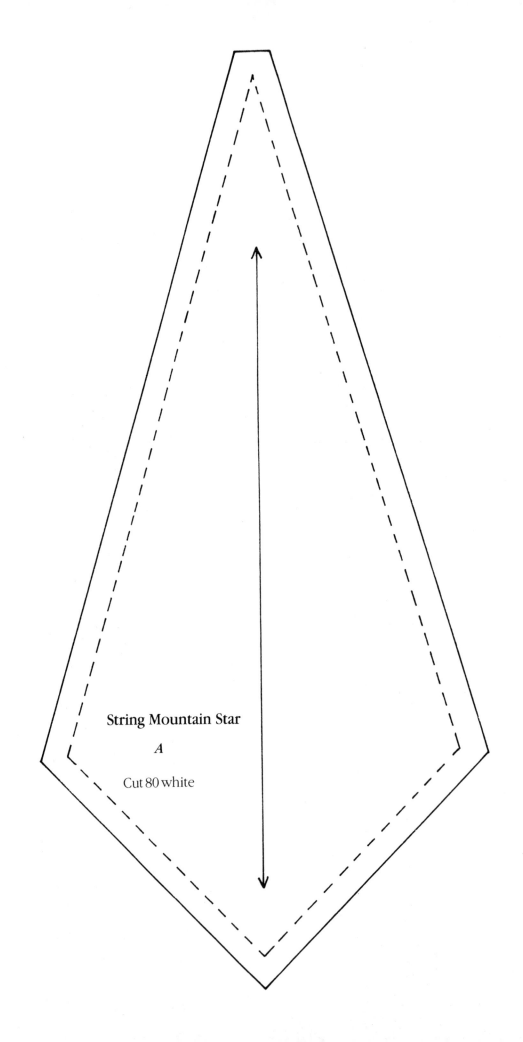

String Mountain Star

A

Cut 80 white

five across and six down. For 30 blocks, add one half of the amount of yardage given above for each piece or strip. Place the quilt top over the lining and batting; quilt as desired. Bind the edges.

Suggested Uses

This easy design is ideal for several different Christmas projects, since it can be quickly made on the sewing machine. Besides making a Christmas quilt, the design might also be used for a nine-block tablecloth or a table runner of just three blocks. Four blocks with borders added can be used as a wall hanging. For a placemat, add 2″-wide borders of white on two sides and 3½″-wide borders on the other two sides of a single block to make a rectangle. Place this over batting and a lining and machine-quilt. Begin quilting in the center of the placemat and work out towards the edges. Quilt across the center of the white wedges, around the white stars, red diamonds and around the edges of the block. Bind the edges in one of the colors used for the strips.

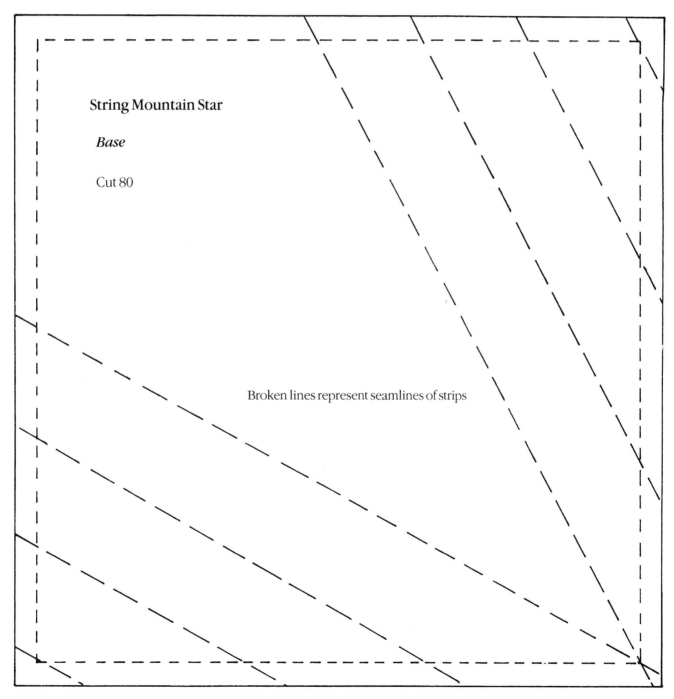

String Mountain Star

Base

Cut 80

Broken lines represent seamlines of strips

McDougall String Quilt

Fig. A. *A four-block setting.*

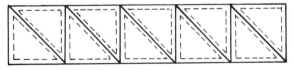

Fig B. *Trace the triangle to the 2⅞″-wide strips and cut with the rotary cutter.*

Method: Strips sewn in sequence to a paper base.

Finished Block Size: 12″. Each block consists of four 6″ square units.

Number of Blocks for Quilt: 42.

Setting: Six blocks across by seven blocks down. An interesting secondary design forms when the blocks are set together without sashing strips between the blocks (*Fig. A*).

Quilt Size: 72″ × 84″ without borders.

Materials for Quilt

Yardage is given below; however, this can be a scrap quilt, with each 12″ block using different fabrics for the strips. For unity, use the same fabric in all the blocks for strip #6. Also, make all of the inside triangles #1A of a single fabric, and all of the corner triangles #1B of a different single fabric.

Note: All of the strips listed below are cut 1½″ wide across the full width of the fabric.

45″-wide fabrics:

    1 yd. solid. Cut 168 inside triangles #1A. See cutting directions below.

    1 yd. print. Cut 168 corner triangles #1B. See cutting directions below.

    2 yds. print for strips #2 and 3. Cut 36 strips.

    2½ yds. print for strips #4 and 5. Cut 56 strips.

    2 yds. solid for strip #6. Cut 42 strips.

    1½ yds. print for strip #7. Cut 30 strips.

    1½ yds. solid for strip #8 (do not use the same fabric as for strip #6). Cut 22 strips.

    6 yds. of fabric for lining.

Newspaper for bases.

Batting.

The #1 triangles are cut by the quick-cut method from strips. Trace the pattern for the triangle, including the seam allowance, and cut a template from lightweight cardboard or plastic. Using the rotary cutter, cut strips 2⅞″ wide. Following *Fig. B*, place the template on the strip and mark the triangles (29 triangles will fit across each strip). Stack several strips together with a marked strip on top and pin. Cut on the vertical and diagonal lines.

For each block, cut four 7″ squares of newspaper (the seam allowance is included in this measurement); cut each square in half diagonally (*Fig. C*).

Mark the center of the longest side of one paper triangle. Center an inside triangle #1A on this side with the long edges matching; pin in place. Following *Fig. D*, add the

26

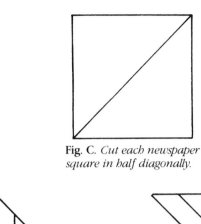

Fig. C. *Cut each newspaper square in half diagonally.*

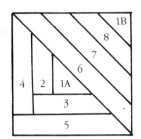

Fig. D.

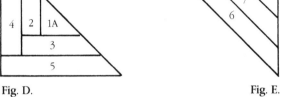

Fig. E.

Fig. F. *Join the triangles to make a square.*

Fig. G. *Four squares joined to make a block.*

#*1*

McDougall String Quilt

A. Cut 168 solid

B. Cut 168 print

strips in numerical order. Do not cut the strips before attaching them to the base, but trim them close to the base after sewing. First, using a ¼″ seam, sew strip #2 to one side of triangle #1A. The end of strip #2 should be even with the edge of #1A. Press the seam, then turn the strip to the right side and press again. Then add strips 3, 4 and 5. When all the strips are in place, turn the piece over and trim the excess fabric even with the edges of the base. Carefully tear away the paper.

On a second paper triangle, sew strip #6 across the longest edge of the triangle, matching the raw edges. Add strips #7 and 8 and corner square #1B *(Fig. E)*. Trim the excess fabric. Carefully tear away the paper. Sew the finished triangles together along the long edges to make a square *(Fig. F)*. Repeat to form four units. Sew the units together so that the #5 strips meet at the center of the block *(Fig. G)*.

Sew the blocks together to form seven rows of six blocks each; sew the rows together. To enlarge the quilt, add borders on all sides. Place the quilt top over the batting and lining; quilt as desired along the strips and triangles. Bind the edges.

Star Magic

Method: Strips sewn to a triangular base with small appliquéd stars at the center of each block.

Finished Block Size: 12″.

Number of Blocks for Wall Quilt: Nine.

Setting: Three blocks across by three blocks down.

Quilt Size: 36″ × 36″ without borders.

Materials for Wall Quilt

Note: Cut all strips listed below 1⅞″ wide across the full width of the fabric.

45″-wide fabrics:

1 yd. medium print for pattern piece #1. Cut 36. See cutting directions below.

1 yd. dark solid for strip #2. Cut 13 strips.

¾ yd. solid for strip #3. Cut nine strips.

¾ yd. light print for strip #4. Cut seven strips.

⅜ yd. light print for pattern piece #5. Cut 36. See cutting directions below.

1¼ yds. fabric for lining.

Newspaper for bases or 2¼ yds. 36″-wide very thin interfacing.

Batting.

Thread to match fabrics.

Four-block setting

On a rectangular sheet of newspaper, mark 13″ from the corner on two adjacent sides. With a ruler and pencil, draw a line connecting the two points. Fold on this line and cut out the square. Fold the square diagonally in the other direction to make four small triangles *(Fig. A)*. Cut along the fold lines. The seam allowances are included in the measurements given. Use these paper triangles as patterns if you are using interfacing for the bases. Four triangular bases will be needed for each block. Mark the center of the long side of each triangle *(Fig. B)*.

Trace the patterns for pieces #1 and 5, including the seam allowances. Cut templates from lightweight cardboard or plastic.

For piece #1, cut three strips 6⅝″ wide across the full width of the fabric. Following *Fig. C,* and being careful to

place the arrow on the template on the straight grain of the fabric, trace the template to the strip (13 pieces should fit across the strip). Stack the strips with the marked strip on top and pin. Cut out the pieces, using scissors to cut the pointed ends. Cut 36 pieces in all.

For piece #5, cut two strips 3″ wide and cut in the same manner.

For each triangle, place piece #1 on the base, matching the points and the centers; pin or baste in place. Right sides together, stitch a #2 strip to each side of piece #1 in a ¼″ seam, sewing through the base. Cut the strip about ½″ beyond the edges of the base. Turn the strip to the right side and press; pin through the seam. Sew strips #3 and 4 to each side in the same way. Turn the piece over and trim the edges of the strip even with the base.

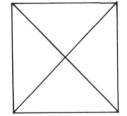

Fig. A. *Fold the newspaper square diagonally to form four small triangles.*

Fig. B. *Mark the center of the long side of each triangle.*

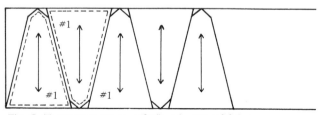

Fig. C. *Trace piece #1 to a 6⅝″-wide strip of fabric.*

Turn under a ¼″ hem on the long edges of piece #5 and baste it in place. To make a sharp point, first fold in the point *(Fig. D)*. Turn under one side, trimming away a small amount of the excess fabric *(Fig. E)*; then turn under the remaining side *(Fig. F)*. Pin the piece at the top of piece #1, matching the raw edges *(Fig. G)*; blindstitch the folded edges. The short edges of piece #5 will be caught in the seams when the triangles are joined. Make four triangles for each block. If paper has been used for the base, remove the paper, being careful not to stretch the bias edges. Machine-stitching ⅛″ from the edges will prevent stretching.

For each block, stitch four triangles together so that the points meet, carefully matching the seams *(Fig. H)*. Sew the blocks together in three rows of three blocks each; sew the rows together. To enlarge the quilt, cut four border strips 4″ wide by 45″ long. Sew the borders to the sides, then the top and bottom. Trim the excess fabric. Place the quilt top over the batting and lining. Quilt as desired and bind the edges.

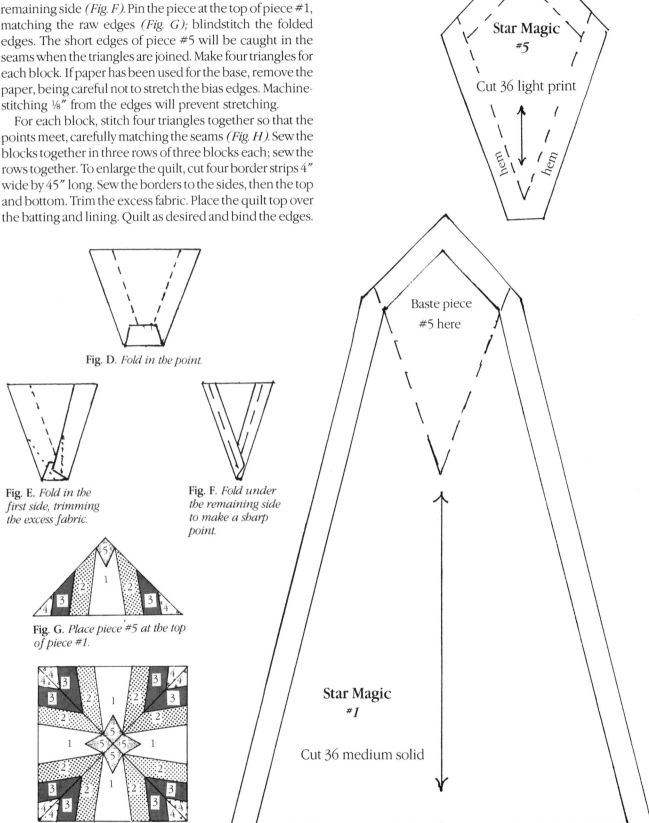

Fig. D. *Fold in the point.*

Fig. E. *Fold in the first side, trimming the excess fabric.*

Fig. F. *Fold under the remaining side to make a sharp point.*

Fig. G. *Place piece #5 at the top of piece #1.*

Fig. H. *Four triangles joined to make a block.*

Star Magic #5

Cut 36 light print

hem   hem

Baste piece #5 here

Star Magic #1

Cut 36 medium solid

Silent Night

Method: Chevron strip-piecing on a shaped base.
Finished Block Size: 16″ × 20″.
Number of Blocks for Quilt: Four.
Quilt Size: 50″ × 58″, including borders.
Materials for Quilt

   Note: To cut the tree strips, first cut 2⁵⁄₁₆″-wide strips across the full width of the fabric (see "Cutting Strips of Odd Widths" on page 2). Trace the templates to the right side of the fabric and cut out the pieces.

   45″-wide fabrics:

   Scrap of solid green or green print #1 for triangle #1 in tree. Cut four.

   ⅓ yd. green print #2 for tree strips #2 and 3. Cut two long strips, then cut four of each tree strip.

   ⅓ yd. green print #3 for tree strips #4 and 5. Cut three long strips, then cut four of each tree strip.

   ½ yd. green print #4 for tree strips #6 and 7. Cut four long strips, then cut four of each tree strip.

   1½ yds. light print for block background pieces #8 and 9. Cut four each of #8, #8 reversed, #9 and #9 reversed.

   Scrap of brown or green for tree trunk #10. Cut four.

   ¼ yd. medium yellow for star #11. Cut two strips 3¾″ wide across the full width of the fabric.

1⅜ yds. each medium blue and dark blue for borders. See cutting instructions below.

3½ yds. lining fabric.

Batting.

Threads to match fabrics.

Newspaper for bases.

Trace patterns for pieces #1–7, 10 and 11. In order to save space, the patterns for strips #4, 5 and 6 are compressed. To make a full pattern for these pieces, trace the strip from the bottom point to the top broken line (see the arrow on the pattern). Move the tracing paper so that this broken line matches the lower broken line on the pattern; the notches should match. Trace the rest of the pattern. The pattern for strip #7 is given in two pieces. Match the broken lines when tracing the pattern. Cut the templates from lightweight cardboard or plastic. The angles at the ends of the tree strips are not the same on each end. The templates must be traced onto the right side of the fabric in order to cut the angles properly. Mark the top end of each strip.

Following *Fig. A,* draw patterns for block background pieces #8 and 9 on a large sheet of newspaper. Cut out all pieces.

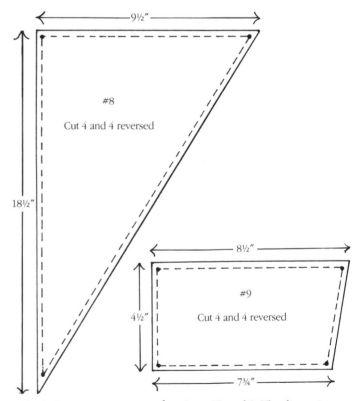

Fig. A. *Draw paper patterns for pieces #8 and 9. The dimensions given include the seam allowances.*

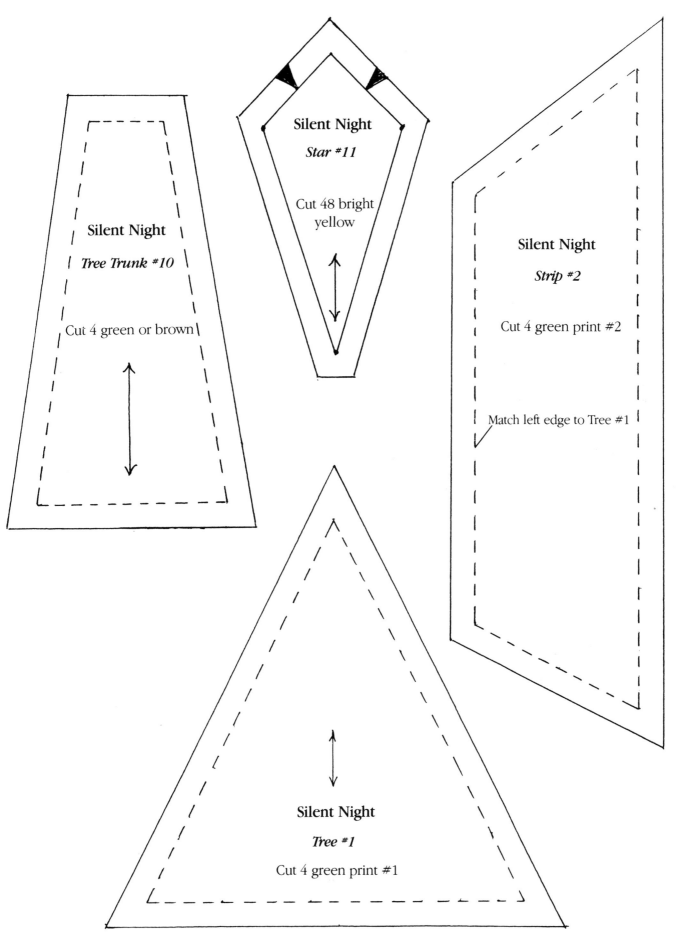

Silent Night

Tree Trunk #10

Cut 4 green or brown

Silent Night

Star #11

Cut 48 bright yellow

Silent Night

Strip #2

Cut 4 green print #2

Match left edge to Tree #1

Silent Night

Tree #1

Cut 4 green print #1

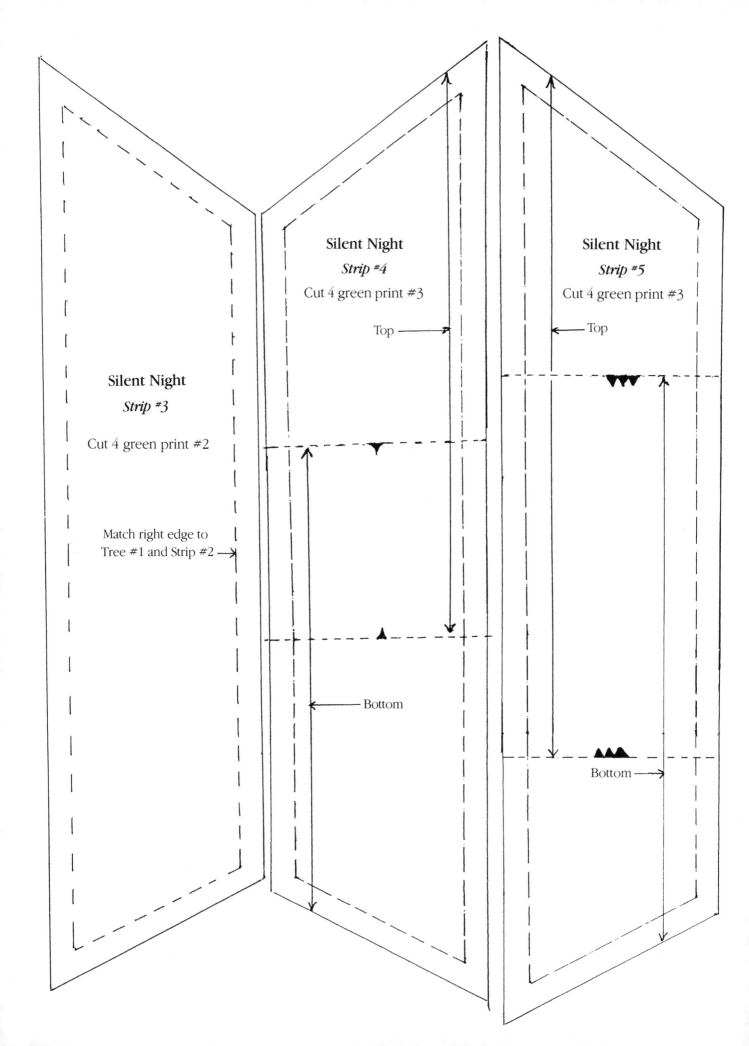

Silent Night

Strip #3

Cut 4 green print #2

Match right edge to
Tree #1 and Strip #2 →

Silent Night

Strip #4

Cut 4 green print #3

Top →

Bottom

Silent Night

Strip #5

Cut 4 green print #3

← Top

Bottom →

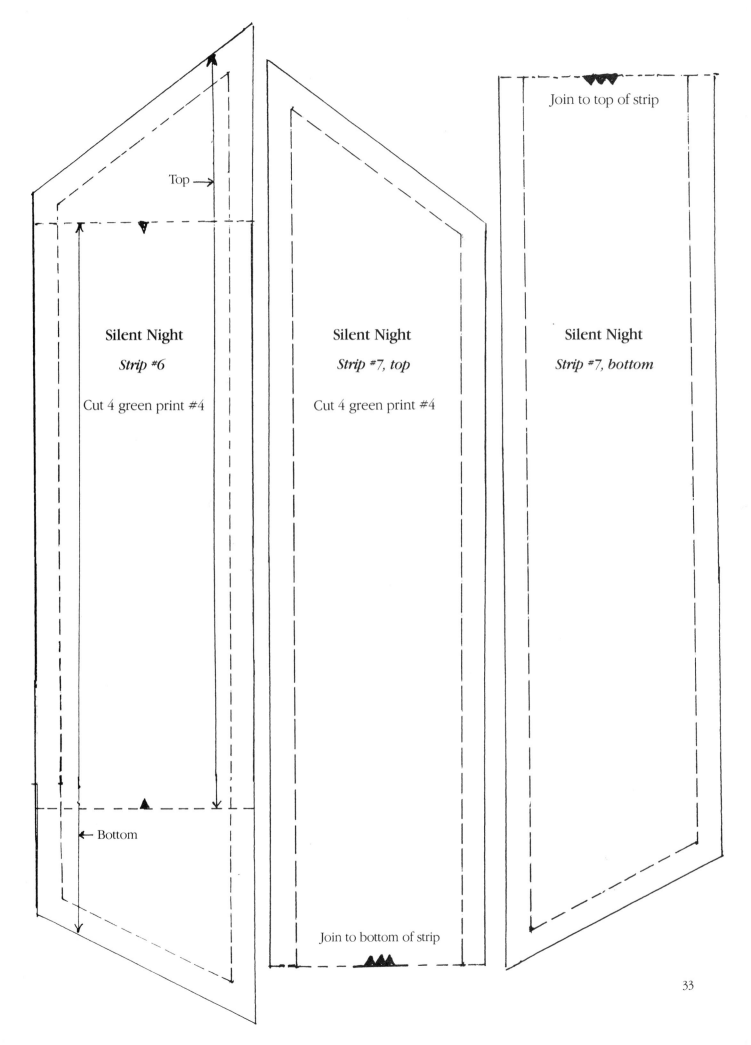

Silent Night

Strip #6

Cut 4 green print #4

Top →

▽

▲

← Bottom

Silent Night

Strip #7, top

Cut 4 green print #4

Join to bottom of strip

▲▲▲

Silent Night

Strip #7, bottom

Join to top of strip

▼▼▼

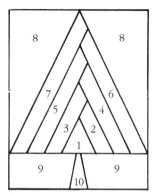

Fig. B. *Sew the strips to the base in numerical order.*

Fig. D. *Join two A sections, alternating the colors.*

Sewing the Tree Blocks

The tree block may be constructed without a base, as can any pieced design; however, using a paper base will stabilize the stitching.

Cut four 16½″ squares of newspaper for bases for the strip piecing. Fold to mark the lengthwise center. For each tree, place triangle #1 over the center line and even with the bottom edge; baste in place. With right sides together, match the short side of strip #2 to the right edge of triangle #1; a tiny ¼″ triangle will extend at each end. Stitch in a ¼″ seam. Press the seam flat as stitched to set the stitches, then turn the strip to the right side and press again. The raw edges should now line up on the left side of triangle #1 and at the bottom. Add strips #1–7 in numerical order following *Fig. B.* As each strip is added, check the edges to keep the block true. When the tree is complete, remove the paper backing. Sew a #9 background piece to each side of a #10 tree trunk. Press the seams and stitch the piece to the lower edge of the tree. Sew a background triangle #8 to each side of the tree. Some trimming of this piece may be necessary. Make sure the top corners form true right angles.

Mark the seamline on the wrong side—it should just cross the tip of the tree. Check to see that the block measures the same on opposite sides and make any necessary adjustments to the marked seamline. Mark the center of each side of the block. Make four tree blocks.

Sashing and Borders

The sashing and borders are made in two shades of blue. The colors reverse at the center of each block; the color-change seams will be covered by appliquéd stars. Refer to *Fig. G* for the placement of the colors in the border.

To cut the sashing and the borders, first remove the selvages from the border fabrics. Cutting the strips on the lengthwise grain, cut eight 3½″-wide strips from each border fabric. Using ¼″ seams, sew the light and dark strips together in pairs along the long edges to form 6½″-wide strips. Following *Fig. C*, cut the strips to the proper length.

Stitch two A sections together as in *Fig. D*; repeat with the other A sections. Sew one of the joined A sections to the side edge of a tree block, adjusting the border so that the seam falls at the center of the block. Sew a second tree block to the other side of the A section. Trim the ends of the strip even with the edges of the block. Sew the other two tree blocks to the other joined A section.

To make the center horizontal sashing, center a B section on the lower edge of one of the joined tree block pieces, matching the dark edge of the border to the raw edge of the tree blocks. Baste, starting and stopping about 1″ short of the center point of each tree block. Pin a C section to each end of the B section, turning it so that the colors are reversed. Adjust the strips so that the seam will fall at the center of the tree trunk and stitch. Baste the C sections to the tree blocks, then stitch across the entire edge. Sew the free edge of this joined strip to the top of the other tree block piece, making sure that the seams fall at the tips of the trees. Trim the ends of the C sections even with the edges of the tree blocks.

In the same way, baste B sections to the top and bottom edges of the joined blocks. The light edge of the B section should be against the blocks. Sew D sections to each end of the B sections, reversing the colors. Baste the D sections to the edges of the blocks. The outer ends of the D sections should extend about 7″ beyond the edges of the quilt to allow for mitering the corners. Stitch the entire seam, starting and stopping exactly on the seamline of the tree

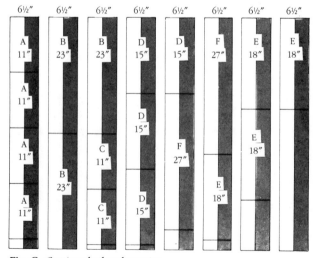

Fig. C. *Cutting the border strips.*

34

blocks at the ends. Secure the seam by backstitching at each end. Attach E and F border sections to the sides of the quilt in the same way. Before stitching the mitered corners, measure the sides against one another to make sure they are the same length; make any necessary adjustments in the seams. Stitch the mitered corners, matching the seams carefully. See page 9 for sewing mitered corners.

Stars

Trace the star template #11 to the yellow strips following *Fig. E;* cut 48 pieces. Stitch the pieces together in pairs along one short edge, matching the notches and beginning and ending at the dots on the template. Sew the pairs together to form 12 stars, starting and stopping at the dots *(Fig. F)*. Turn under and baste a ¼″ hem on all edges of the stars. See page 29 for making a sharp point. Pin a star over each color-change seam in the border; blindstitch in place *(Fig. G)*. Take several tiny stitches very close together at each point and angle to fasten securely.

Place the quilt top over the batting and lining and quilt as desired. Bind the edges.

Fig. F. *Make 12 stars.*

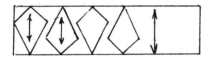

Fig. E. *Trace the star template to 3¾″-wide strips of fabric.*

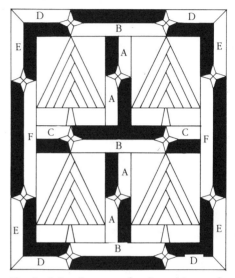

Fig. G. *Color placement for the sashing and borders.*

Hit or Miss

Method: Strips sewn to a shaped base.
Finished Block Size: 13¾″.
Number of Blocks for Quilt: 35.
Setting: Five blocks across by seven down.
Quilt Size: Approximately 69″ × 96″ without borders.
Materials for Quilt
    2 yds. 45″-wide medium color fabric for center bars.
    Scraps of various colors and prints for strips.
    5 yds. fabric for lining.
    Newspaper for bases.
    Batting.
    Thread.

This is an easy scrap quilt for using up all the small pieces in the scrapbag.

To make the pattern for the base, measure 15″ across one edge of a sheet of newspaper; mark the center. Measure 7½″ straight up from the center to mark the apex of the triangle. Draw lines from the apex to the ends of the base. These measurements include the seam allowance. Cut a

cardboard template for the base. Stack four layers of newspaper and mark and cut four triangles at a time for each block.

Using the rotary cutter, cut the center bars 3″ wide. From scraps, cut strips of various widths. Do not cut the strips to length until they are sewn to the base. For each triangle, place the center bar over the center of the base, letting the strip extend over the edges. Cut the ends about ½″ from the edges. With right sides together, taking a ¼″ seam, sew random strips to each side of the center bar until the base is completely covered. As each strip is joined, turn it to the right side and press, then pin through the seam. When the base is covered, turn the piece over and trim the strips even with the edges of the base. Make four triangles for each block. Sew the triangles together so that the points meet at the center of the block. Remove the paper.

Sew the blocks together in seven rows of five blocks each. Sew the rows together. Place the quilt top over the batting and lining; quilt as desired. Bind the edges.

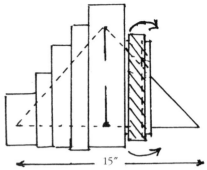

Fig. A. *Sew strips to either side of the center bar.*

Log Cabin
Rocky Road to Kansas

Method: Strips sewn to a shaped base.
Finished Block Size: 13¾″.
Number of Blocks for Quilt: 30.
Setting: Five blocks across by six blocks down, without sashing strips.
Quilt Size: Approximately 69″ × 82″. Add 4″-wide borders on all sides to increase the size to 77″ × 90″.

To make the wall hanging shown in the photograph, see the instructions at the end.

Materials for Quilt
Note: Strips #1–9 are cut 1½″ wide across the full width of the fabric. Cutting to length is done after the strips are sewn to the base.

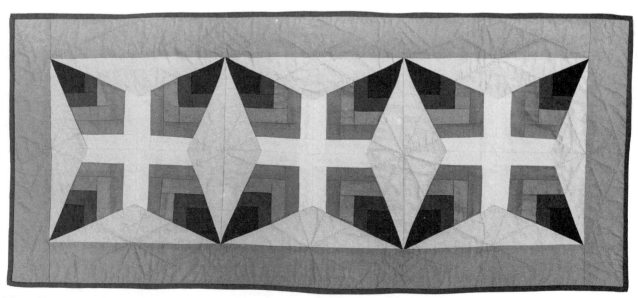

Three-block wall hanging

45″-wide fabrics:

1⅓ yds. red solid for piece #1. Cut 120 pieces from six strips cut 4¾″ wide across the full width of the fabric.

1 yd. purple solid. Cut 16 long strips for #2 and 3 strips.

1 yd. green solid. Cut 19 long strips for #4 and 5 strips.

1⅓ yds. rose solid. Cut 24 long strips for #6 and 7 strips.

1½ yds. yellow solid. Cut 27 long strips for #8 and 9 strips.

2½ yds. medium aqua for B pieces. Cut 120 pieces from 24 strips cut 3½″ wide across the full width of the fabric.

7½ yds. lining fabric.

2½ yds. fabric for borders (optional).

5½ yds. 36″-wide very thin interfacing for A bases. Cut 120 bases from 18 strips cut 10⅝″ wide across the full width of the fabric. *Note:* Newspaper can also be used for the bases.

Batting.

Thread.

Trace patterns for pieces #1, A and B, including seam allowances. To make a full pattern for piece B, trace it to the folded edge of the paper and cut it out. Cut templates from lightweight cardboard or plastic. Following *Figs. A, B* and *C*, trace the templates to the fabric strips and cut out the pieces.

For each point, place piece #1 on the long end of the point base A. With right sides together, sew strip #2 to the left-hand edge of piece #1. Turn the strip to the right side and finger-press. Pin through the seam. Trim one end of the strip even with the top of piece #1 and the other end about ½″ beyond the edge of the base. Attach strip #3 to the top of pieces #1 and #2. Continue to sew on strips in numerical order, following *Fig. D* until the base is covered. Turn the piece over and trim the ends of the strips even with the edges of the base. Make four points for each block.

Sew the points together in pairs along one short edge, starting and stopping exactly on the seamline. Sew the pairs together to form a star. Right sides together, pin a B piece to the star, pinning one side only from the center to the point of the star. Stitch, starting and stopping exactly on the seamline. Sew the second side from the center out. Repeat on each side of the star. Make 30 blocks.

Join the blocks in six rows of five blocks each. Join the rows. If desired, cut two side borders 4½″ × 84″ and two top and bottom borders 4½″ × 77″. Sew the borders to the sides, then the top and bottom, of the quilt.

Place the quilt top over the batting and lining; quilt as desired. Bind the edges.

Three-Block Wall Hanging

Make three blocks as described above; sew the blocks together to form a strip. Cut two borders 4½″ × 42″ and two borders 4½″ × 23″. Sew borders to the long edges, then to the ends of the hanging. Place the hanging over the batting and lining; quilt as desired. Bind the edges.

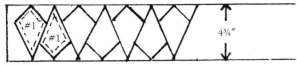

Fig. A. *Trace piece #1 twenty times across each fabric strip and cut out.*

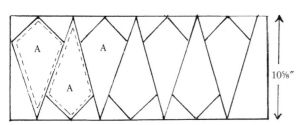

Fig. B. *Trace base A seven times across each interfacing strip and cut out.*

Fig. C. *Trace B triangle five times across each fabric strip and cut out.*

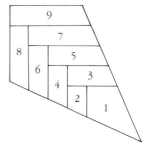

Fig. D. *Sew the strips to the base in numerical order.*

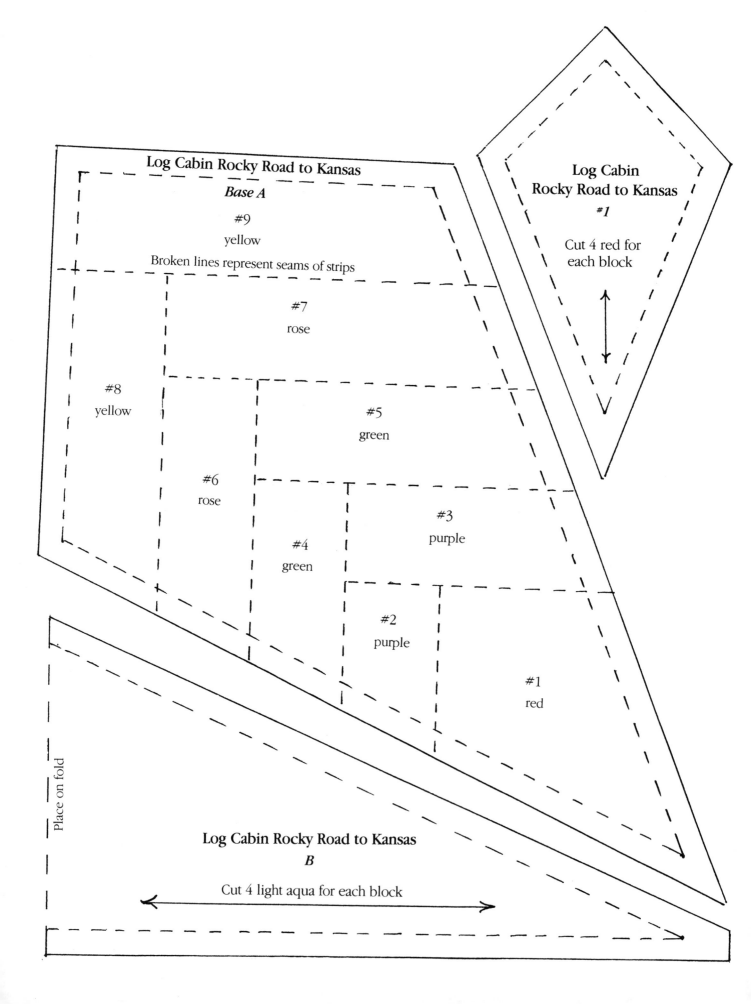

Log Cabin Rocky Road to Kansas

Base A

#9
yellow

Broken lines represent seams of strips

#7
rose

#8
yellow

#5
green

#6
rose

#4
green

#3
purple

#2
purple

#1
red

**Log Cabin
Rocky Road to Kansas**

#1

Cut 4 red for
each block

Place on fold

Log Cabin Rocky Road to Kansas
B

Cut 4 light aqua for each block

Stars in Stripes

Method: Strips sewn onto a diamond-shaped base, then pieced into a square block.

Finished Block Size: 14″.

Number of Blocks for Quilt: 20.

Setting: Four blocks across by five down, with 2″-wide sashing strips between blocks.

Quilt Size: 74″ × 90″, including sashing strips and 4″-wide borders.

Materials for Quilt

45″-wide fabrics:

1 yd. dark solid for strip #1. Cut 17 strips 1½″ wide across the full width of the fabric.

1¾ yds. dark solid for strip #4 (this can be the same fabric as #1). Cut 18 strips 2½″ wide across the full width of the fabric.

1½ yds. light print for strip #2. Cut 32 strips 1½″ wide across the full width of the fabric.

1½ yds. medium solid for strip #3. Cut 26 strips 1½″ wide across the full width of the fabric.

2½ yds. light solid for pieces B and C. Cut 80 of each piece; see cutting instructions below.

1½ yds. contrasting solid or print for E sashing strips. Cut 49. See cutting instructions below.

¼ yd. print or solid for D corner squares. Cut 30; see cutting instructions below.

2½ yds. border fabric. Cut two side borders 4½″ × 84″; two end borders 4½″ × 78″. (Extra length is included for take-up in sewing; trim borders to the proper length after attaching them.)

5½ yds. lining fabric.

Newspaper or 3 yds. 36″-wide very thin interfacing for A diamond bases.

Batting.

Trace patterns for pieces A, B and C including seam allowances. Cut templates from lightweight cardboard or plastic. Cut 160 A bases from newspaper, or cut 27 strips 3½″ wide across the full width of the interfacing. Trace template A six times across one strip *(Fig. A);* stack the strips and cut out the pieces.

Make the strip-pieced diamonds in pairs, turning one base over before adding the strips, so that strip #1 will match up straight across *(Fig. B).* Begin by pinning strip #1 across the center of the base. Add strip #2 on each side, taking a ¼″ seam. Turn to the right side and finger press. Pin through the seam. Cut the ends of the strips about ½″ beyond the edges of the base. Add strips #3 and 4. Turn the diamond to the wrong side and trim the fabric even with the edges of the base. If newspaper bases were used, remove the paper.

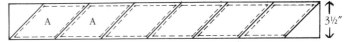

Fig. A. *Trace template A six times across each interfacing strip and cut out.*

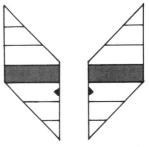

Fig. B. *Make the strip-pieced diamonds in pairs.*

On the back of the diamonds, draw the ¼″ seam allowance. Make a dot where the seamlines intersect.

Sew the diamonds together in pairs along the notched edge, matching the seams and starting and stopping the stitching at the dots. Carefully matching the seams, sew two pairs together to form half-stars; press the seams to one side. Sew the halves together to complete the star. In the center, fan the seam allowances out and press.

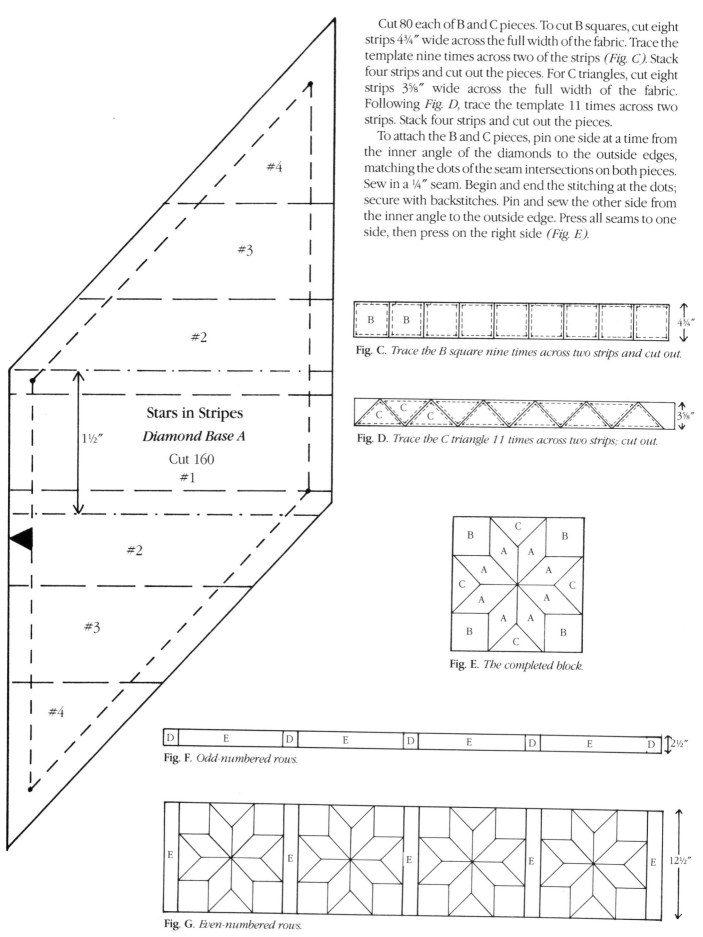

Cut 80 each of B and C pieces. To cut B squares, cut eight strips 4¾" wide across the full width of the fabric. Trace the template nine times across two of the strips *(Fig. C)*. Stack four strips and cut out the pieces. For C triangles, cut eight strips 3⅝" wide across the full width of the fabric. Following *Fig. D,* trace the template 11 times across two strips. Stack four strips and cut out the pieces.

To attach the B and C pieces, pin one side at a time from the inner angle of the diamonds to the outside edges, matching the dots of the seam intersections on both pieces. Sew in a ¼" seam. Begin and end the stitching at the dots; secure with backstitches. Pin and sew the other side from the inner angle to the outside edge. Press all seams to one side, then press on the right side *(Fig. E)*.

Stars in Stripes

Diamond Base A

Cut 160

1½"

#1 #2 #3 #4

Fig. C. *Trace the B square nine times across two strips and cut out.*

4¾"

Fig. D. *Trace the C triangle 11 times across two strips; cut out.*

3⅝"

Fig. E. *The completed block.*

Fig. F. *Odd-numbered rows.*

2½"

Fig. G. *Even-numbered rows.*

12½"

To cut 30 D corner squares, cut two strips 2½" wide across the full width of the fabric; cut strips into 2½" squares. To cut 49 E sashing strips, first cut 17 strips 2½" wide along the lengthwise grain of the fabric. Cut each strip into three 15" long pieces.

To assemble the blocks, make 11 horizontal rows as follows. *Odd-numbered rows:* Starting with a D corner square, sew five corner squares and four E sashing strips together end to end *(Fig. F)*. *Even-numbered rows:* Starting with an E sashing strip, sew five sashing strips and four blocks together *(Fig. G)*. Join the rows, carefully matching the seams *(Fig. H)*.

Sew the borders to the sides, then the top and bottom. Place the quilt top over the batting and lining; quilt as desired. Bind the edges, using the border fabric.

Fig. H. *The quilt top before adding the borders.*

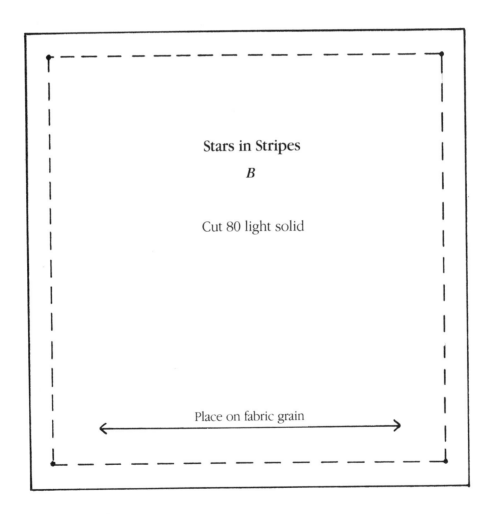

Stars in Stripes

B

Cut 80 light solid

Place on fabric grain

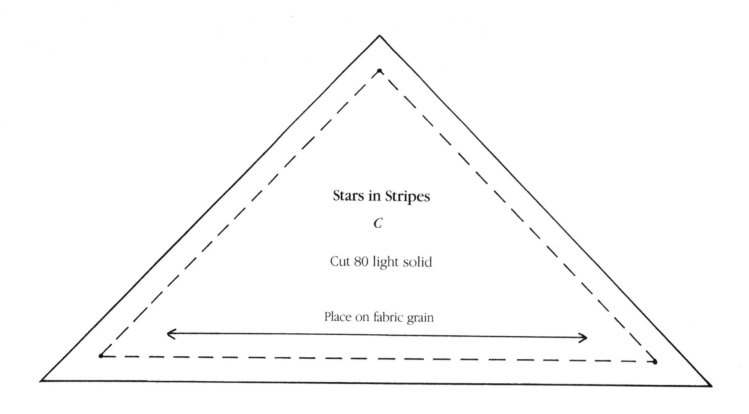

Stars in Stripes

C

Cut 80 light solid

Place on fabric grain

Twin Sisters

Method: Strips sewn to a triangular-shaped base.
Finished Block Size: 12″.
Number of Blocks for Quilt: 42.
Setting: Six blocks across by seven blocks down.
Size of Quilt: 72″ × 84″ without borders.
Materials for Quilt

  Note: All strips listed below are cut 2″ wide across the full
  width of the fabric.
  45″-wide fabrics:
    2⅔ yds. dark blue. Cut 84 #1 triangles. See cutting
      instructions below. Cut 21 strips for strip #4.
    2⅔ yds. rose. Cut 84 #1 triangles. See cutting instruc-
      tions below. Cut 21 strips for strip #4.
    2 yds. blue print. Cut 31 strips for strips #2 and 3.
    2 yds. rose print. Cut 31 strips for strips #2 and 3.
    5 yds. lining fabric.
  Batting.
  Newspaper for bases.

This is a very easy design made on a triangular base. The
fabrics suggested are for a planned color scheme, but scrap
fabrics may also be used.

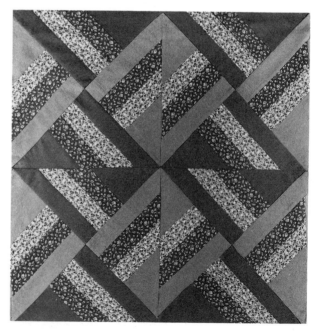

Four-block setting

On a rectangular piece of newspaper, mark 13½″ from the corner on two adjacent sides. With a ruler and pencil draw a line connecting the points. Fold on this line and pin together; cut out the square. Fold the square diagonally in the other direction to make four small triangles and cut along the fold lines. Seam allowances have been included in these measurements. Cut four triangles for each block—a total of 168. The longest side of the triangle will be the outside of the block.

Trace the pattern for the #1 triangle including the seam allowance; cut a template from lightweight cardboard or plastic. Cut 84 triangles each from dark blue and rose fabric. To cut the triangles with the rotary cutter, cut six strips 5″ wide across the full width of the fabric. Cut 5″ squares from each strip, then cut each square in half diagonally *(Fig. A)*.

The triangles are made in two counter-change color schemes as in *Figs. B* and *C.* To make each triangle, pin the #1 triangle in the left corner of the base; add the strips in order, taking a ¼″ seam allowance. The ends of the strips should extend about ½″ beyond the edges of the base. As each strip is sewn in place, turn it to the right side and finger-press; pin through the seam to flatten it. When all the strips have been attached, turn the triangle over and trim the strips even with the edges of the base. Make two blue and two rose triangles for each block. Remove the paper bases.

Sew the blue and rose triangles together in pairs as in *Fig. D.* Sew the pairs together, carefully matching the seams *(Fig. E)*.

Join the blocks in seven rows of six blocks each; sew the rows together. If desired, add borders to enlarge the quilt. Place the quilt top over batting and lining; quilt as desired. Bind the edges.

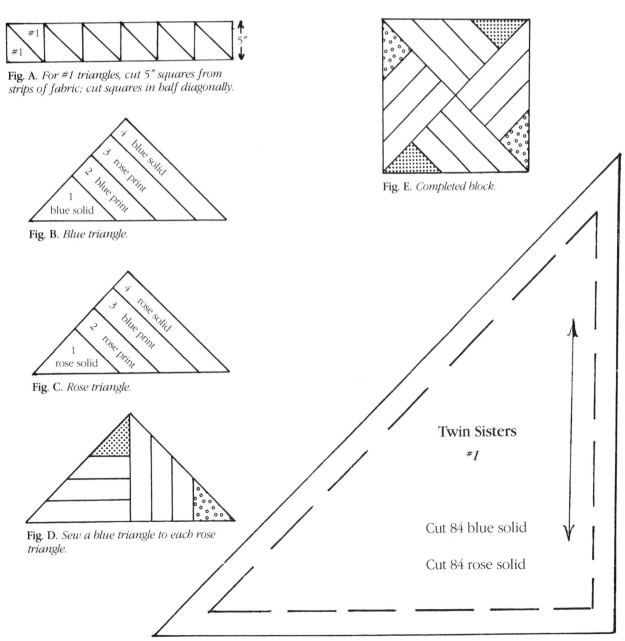

Fig. A. *For #1 triangles, cut 5″ squares from strips of fabric; cut squares in half diagonally.*

Fig. B. *Blue triangle.*

Fig. C. *Rose triangle.*

Fig. D. *Sew a blue triangle to each rose triangle.*

Fig. E. *Completed block.*

Twin Sisters

#1

Cut 84 blue solid

Cut 84 rose solid

IV.

Traditional Designs in Strips Using Method 1 and Method 2

You will recognize the following group of patterns as traditional designs that have been given a new look with strip-pieced sections. Look through your pattern collection and quilt magazines to find others that can be given an individual touch with strip-piecing. The sections may be squares, triangles, diamonds, odd-shaped centers or even background pieces of the design.

Decide if you want a planned color placement and strips of even widths, or if you want the scrap look achieved by using odd widths, prints and all colors in the strips. Solid colors will give a formal feeling, while prints give an informal or country touch. Prints and solids can also be combined effectively.

The strip-pieced sections can be made by cutting them from strip-pieced materials (see Chapter II) or by sewing the strips to a shaped base (see Chapter III).

In order to show how the pieces fit together, the patterns in this chapter are drawn without seam allowances. Be sure to add ¼″ seam allowances around all pieces when making your templates.

Since these blocks are merely examples of how strip-piecing may be used in traditional designs, no yardage requirements are given. To plan the amount of fabric needed for a specific project, see page 5.

Sylvia's Choice

Method: Pieces cut from strip-pieced material.
Finished Block Size: 14″.

This traditional design is from *Hearth and Home* magazine. The strip-pieced sections give it a very different look.

Trace individual patterns for pieces A, B, C and D, adding ¼″ seam allowances around. The arrows indicate the straight grain of the fabric. Cut templates from lightweight cardboard or plastic.

Half of the A and C pieces in each block are cut from strip-pieced material. For a structured look, cut all of the strips 1½″ wide. Trace three A and three C pieces to the material, placing the templates so that the lines in the template are parallel to the seams in the material. Cut out the pieces, cutting only one layer of fabric at a time. Cut three A, three B and three B reversed pieces from light solid fabric; three C, three B and three B reversed pieces from dark solid fabric and four D pieces from light print fabric.

Sew a strip-pieced A wedge to each side of a solid A wedge to form a half-hexagon (*Fig. A*). Sew the remaining solid A wedges to each side of the remaining strip-pieced A

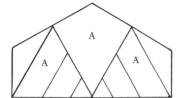

Fig. A. *Join three A wedges to form a half-hexagon.*

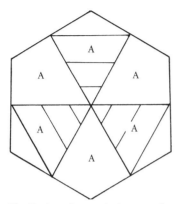

Fig. B. *Sew the two halves together.*

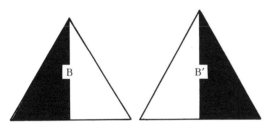

Fig. C. *Make three B and three B′ points.*

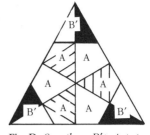

Fig. D. *Sew three B′ points to the center hexagon to form a triangle.*

Fig. E. *Sew a C section to each side of a B triangle.*

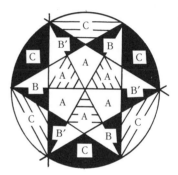

Fig. F. *Sew joined C/B pieces to the center to form a circle.*

wedge. Press the seams to one side. Sew the two halves together along the long straight edge, carefully matching the points *(Fig. B)*.

Join the light and dark B triangles together in pairs to form three B and three B′ points *(Fig. C)*. Sew a B′ point to every other edge of the center hexagon to form a triangle *(Fig. D)*. The dark half of each point should be over a light A wedge.

Sew a strip-pieced C section to the dark edge of a B point; sew a solid C section to the other side of the point *(Fig. E)*. Repeat with remaining C and B pieces to make three identical sections. Sew one of these sections to each side of the center triangle to form a circle *(Fig. F)*.

Baste the D corners to the circle, matching the notches and starting and stopping about 1″ from the ends of the D sections. Pin the ends of the D sections together, adjusting them so that the block lies flat and the seams fall either at the points or in the center of a C section. Stitch the ends together, then stitch the D corners to the circle *(Fig. G)*. Clip the seam allowances and press them toward the D corners.

Fig. G. *Sew the D corners to the circle to complete the block.*

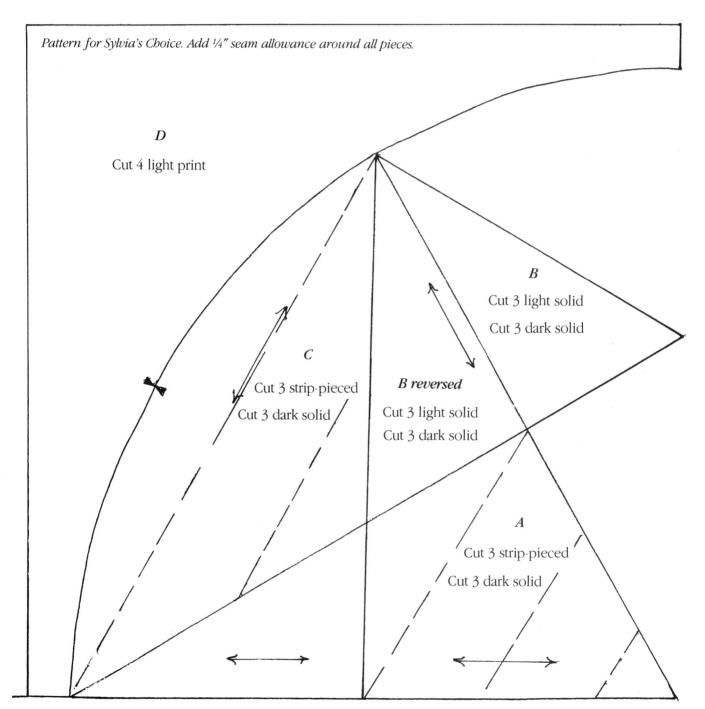

Pattern for Sylvia's Choice. Add ¼″ seam allowance around all pieces.

D

Cut 4 light print

B

Cut 3 light solid

Cut 3 dark solid

C

Cut 3 strip-pieced

Cut 3 dark solid

B reversed

Cut 3 light solid

Cut 3 dark solid

A

Cut 3 strip-pieced

Cut 3 dark solid

Chuck-A-Luck

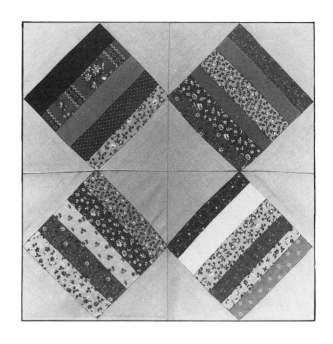

Method 1: Center squares cut from strip-pieced material.
Method 2: Strips sewn to a square base.
Finished Block Size: 12″. Each block is made up of four squares sewn together.

Trace individual patterns for pieces A and B, adding ¼″ seam allowance around. The arrows indicate the straight grain of the fabric. Cut templates from lightweight cardboard or plastic. The lines on Template A indicate the seamlines of the strips.

Pattern for Chuck-a-Luck. Add ¼″ seam allowance around all pieces.

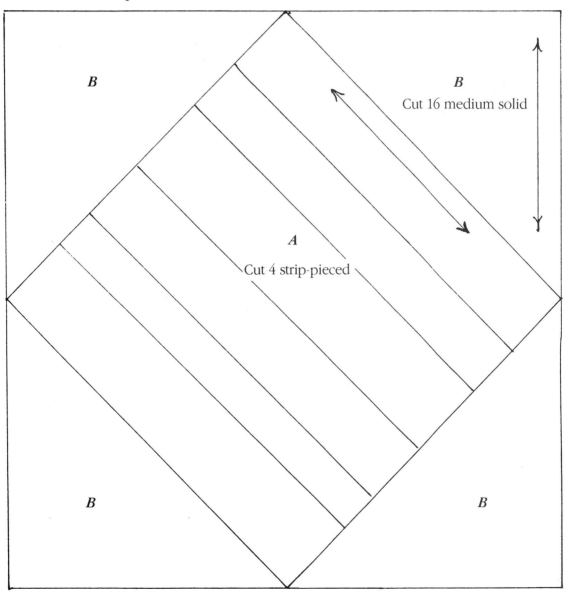

B

B
Cut 16 medium solid

A
Cut 4 strip-pieced

B

B

For method 1, make strip-pieced material and cut four A squares for each block. For method 2, cut four bases for A from newspaper or very thin interfacing; sew strips to the base as described on page 22. When all of the strips have been attached, turn the square over and trim the fabric even with the edges of the base. If paper was used, carefully tear it away.

For each block, cut 16 B triangles from solid fabric. Sew a B triangle to each corner of each A square. Sew four squares together as in the photograph to complete the block.

Comet Star

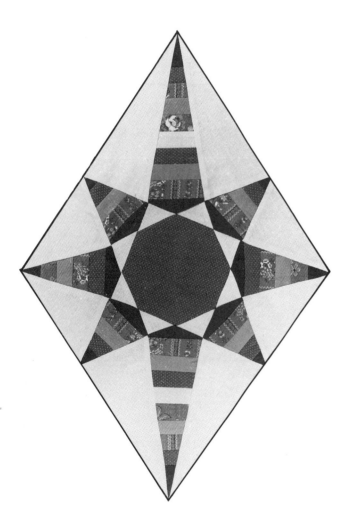

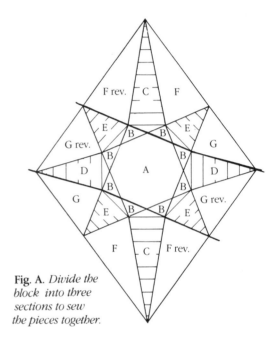

Fig. A. *Divide the block into three sections to sew the pieces together.*

Method: Strips sewn to a shaped base.
Finished Block Size: 18″ by 26″ (measured from point to point).

This traditional design appeared in *Hearth and Home* magazine many years ago. The strip-pieced star points drastically change the look of the design. Use a single block as the central medallion for a quilt, or set the blocks side by side.

Trace individual patterns for pieces A–G, adding ¼″ seam allowances to all edges. Mark the points where the seamlines intersect with dots. The arrows indicate the straight grain of the fabric. Cut templates from lightweight cardboard or plastic.

From newspaper, cut bases for two C, two D and four E points. Cut strips 1½″ wide. Starting at the wider end of each point with a dark strip, sew the strips across the bases as described on page 22. End each point at the narrow end with the same dark fabric to accent the block. The strips should be placed parallel to the lines on the pattern. When all the strips have been attached, turn the pieces over and trim the fabric even with the edge of the bases. Carefully tear away the paper.

Cut one A octagon from medium solid fabric; cut eight B, two F, two F reversed, two G and two G reversed pieces from light solid fabric. Mark the seamlines on the wrong side of all pieces.

Lay out all the pieces of the block as shown in *Fig. A.* Divide the piecing into three sections as indicated by the two heavy lines, so that these sections can be joined in straight ¼″ seams. Be sure to begin and end all seams exactly on the seamlines (where the seams intersect).

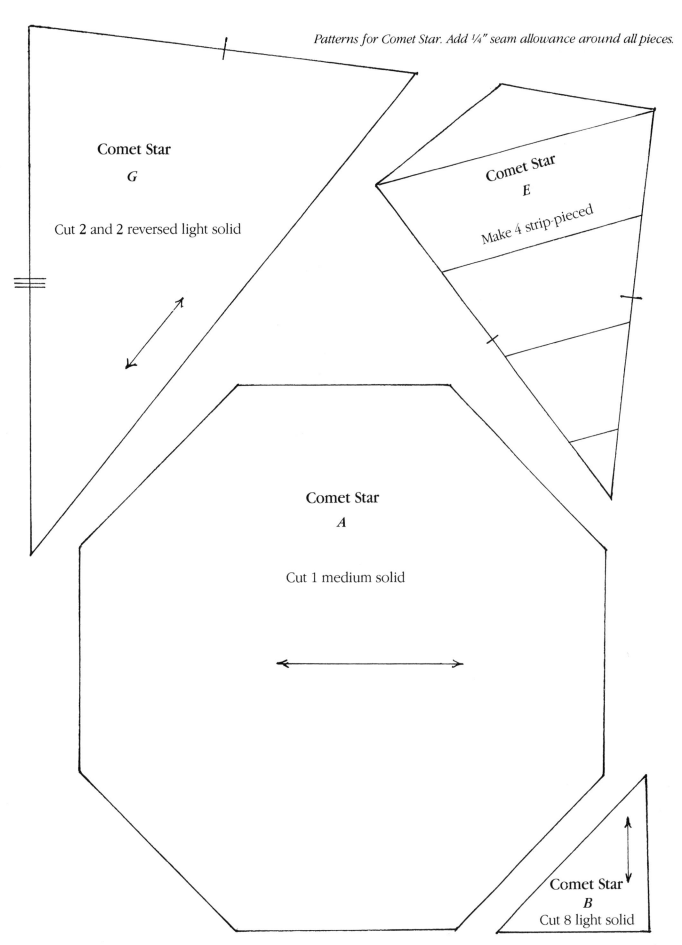

Patterns for Comet Star. Add ¼" seam allowance around all pieces.

Comet Star

G

Cut **2** and **2** reversed light solid

Comet Star

E

Make 4 strip-pieced

Comet Star

A

Cut 1 medium solid

Comet Star

B

Cut 8 light solid

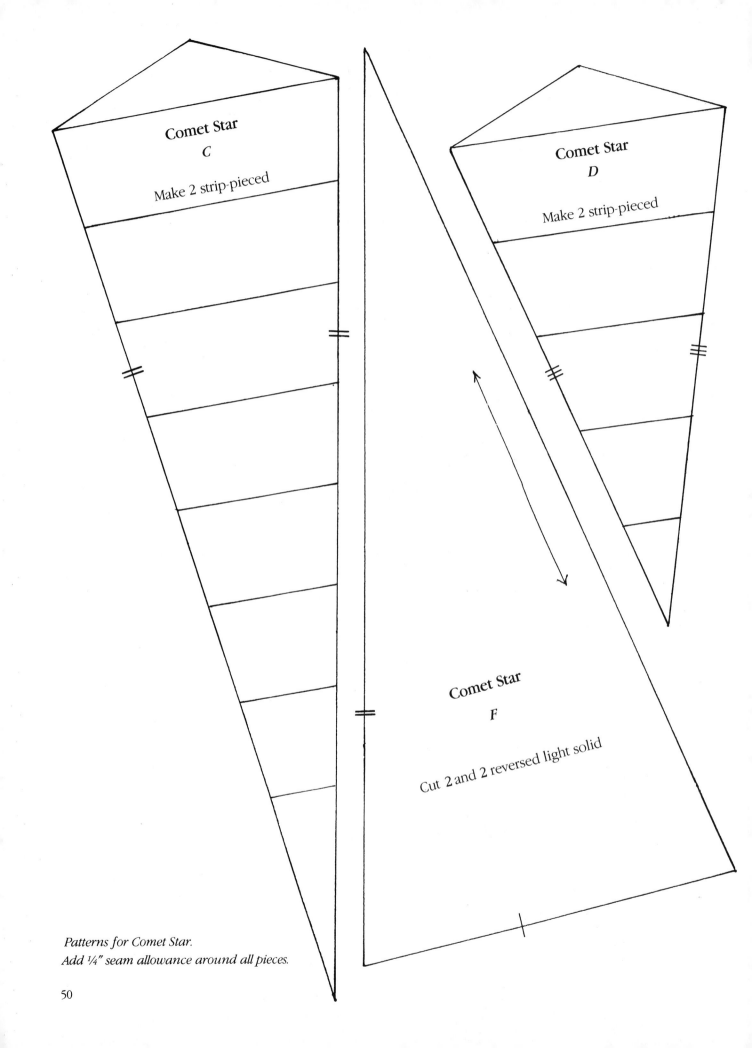

Comet Star
C

Make 2 strip-pieced

Comet Star
D

Make 2 strip-pieced

Comet Star

F

Cut 2 and 2 reversed light solid

Patterns for Comet Star.
Add ¼" seam allowance around all pieces.

Turkey Tracks

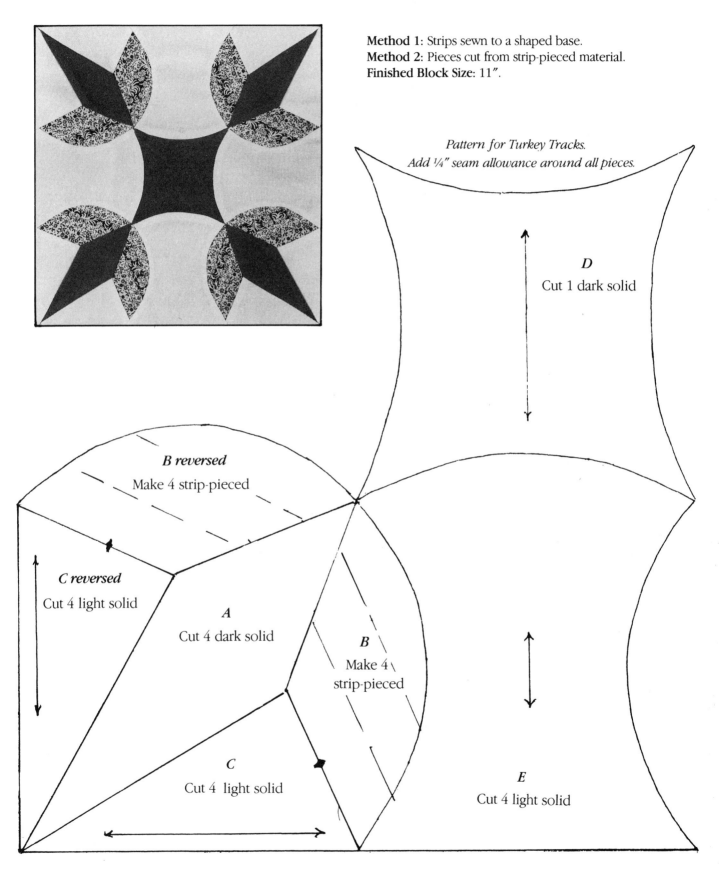

Method 1: Strips sewn to a shaped base.
Method 2: Pieces cut from strip-pieced material.
Finished Block Size: 11″.

Pattern for Turkey Tracks.
Add ¼″ seam allowance around all pieces.

D
Cut 1 dark solid

B reversed
Make 4 strip-pieced

C reversed
Cut 4 light solid

A
Cut 4 dark solid

B
Make 4
strip-pieced

C
Cut 4 light solid

E
Cut 4 light solid

Trace individual patterns for pieces A, B, C, D and E, adding ¼″ seam allowances around. Mark the points where the seamlines intersect with dots. The arrows on the patterns indicate the straight grain of the fabric. Cut templates from lightweight cardboard or plastic.

For method 1, cut bases from newspaper or thin interfacing for four B and four B reversed pieces. Cut strips 1″ to 1⅛″ wide and sew them across the bases as described on page 22. The lines on the patterns indicate the direction of the seams. When all the strips have been added, turn the pieces over and trim the strips even with the edges of the base. If paper has been used, tear it away carefully. For method 2, cut four B and four B reversed pieces from strip-pieced material.

For each block, cut four A pieces and one D piece from dark solid fabric and four C, four C reversed and four E pieces from light solid fabric.

Starting and stopping exactly on the dots at the seam intersections, carefully sew the pieces together as in *Fig. A*. Clip the seam allowances as needed and press the seams towards the darker pieces.

Turkey Tracks may be set with alternate plain blocks. There must be an odd number of blocks both across and down.

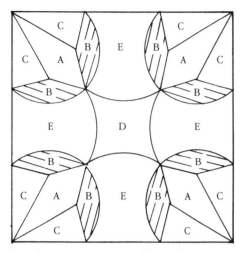

Fig. A. *Join pieces A–E to form the block.*

Rainy Day Rainbows

Method: Strips sewn to a shaped base.
Finished Block Size: 9½″.

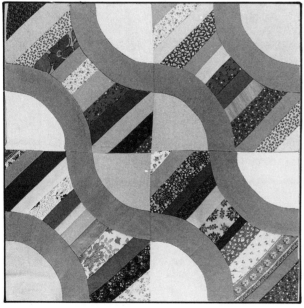

Four-block setting

Turn a rainy day into rainbows by putting the scrapbag beside the sewing machine and attaching random-width strips in a rainbow of colors to bases cut from thin interfacing or newspaper.

This pattern has several other "cousins"—Rainbow, Drunkard's Trail, Railroad Around Rocky Mountain, Rattlesnake and Snake Trail.

Trace individual patterns for pieces A, B and C, adding ¼″ seam allowances to all curved edges. Make full patterns by placing the patterns on the fold of the paper and cutting them out. Cut templates from lightweight cardboard or plastic.

Cut bases for C pieces from newspaper or lightweight interfacing. Sew strips of various widths and colors to the bases as described on page 22. The lines on the pattern should be parallel to the seams of the strips. When all of the strips have been attached, turn the piece over and trim the fabric even with the edges of the base. If paper has been used, tear it away carefully.

Cut two A and two B pieces for each block from solid fabric. Sew a B band to each side of the C section, matching the notches and centers. Clip the seam allowances at

Pattern for Rainy Day Rainbows. Trace the pieces to folded paper to make full patterns.
Add ¼" seam allowance to all curved edges.

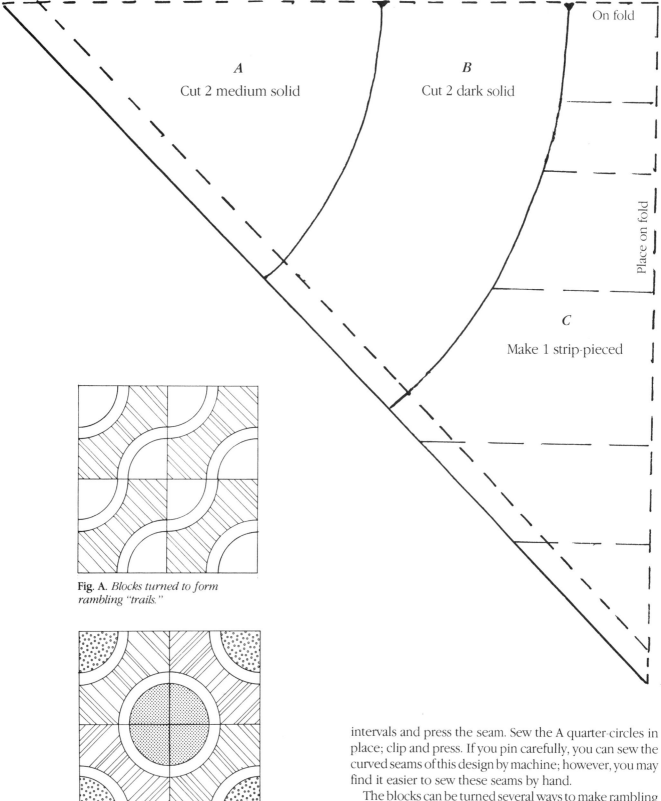

A
Cut 2 medium solid

B
Cut 2 dark solid

On fold

Place on fold

C
Make 1 strip-pieced

Fig. A. *Blocks turned to form rambling "trails."*

Fig. B. *Blocks turned to form banded circles.*

intervals and press the seam. Sew the A quarter-circles in place; clip and press. If you pin carefully, you can sew the curved seams of this design by machine; however, you may find it easier to sew these seams by hand.

The blocks can be turned several ways to make rambling trails as in *Fig. A,* or the quarter-circles can be matched to create banded circles. This is especially effective if two colors are used for the A pieces *(Fig. B).*

Improved Nine-Patch

Method: Strips sewn to a shaped base.
Finished Block Size: 12″.

You may recognize this old favorite by some of its other names—Nine Patch Variation or Glorified Nine Patch, for example. This version uses strips for pieces A and C. You could also use strips for D *(Fig. A)*. Interesting things happen when the blocks are set side by side.

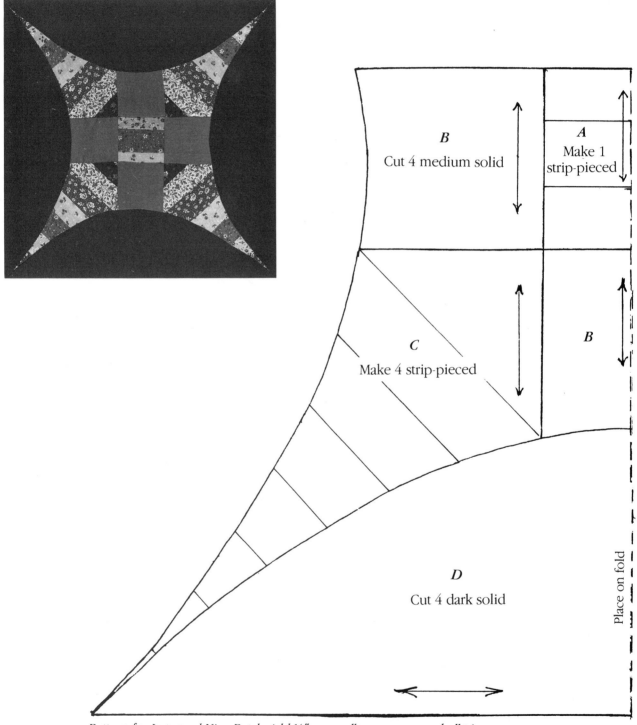

Pattern for Improved Nine-Patch. Add ¼″ seam allowance around all pieces.

Trace individual patterns for pieces A, B, C and D, adding ¼″ seam allowances around. To make complete patterns for A and D, trace them to the folded edge of a piece of paper and cut them out. The arrows on the patterns indicate the straight grain of the fabric. Cut templates from lightweight cardboard or plastic.

For each block, cut four bases for piece C and one base for piece A from newspaper or thin interfacing. Cut strips 1¼″ wide; sew them to the bases as described on page 22. The lines in the pattern indicate the seams of the strips. After the strips have been attached, turn the pieces over and trim the fabric even with the edges of the bases. If paper has been used, carefully tear it away.

Cut four B pieces from medium solid fabric and four D pieces from dark solid fabric.

Arrange the A, B and C pieces following *Fig. B.* Sew the pieces together in rows, then sew the rows together. Baste the D pieces to the center, matching the notches and clipping the seam allowances as needed. Stitch the seams, being very careful to sew the long, thin points of the C pieces accurately.

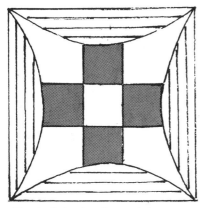

Fig. A. *Strip-pieced material used for the outside pieces.*

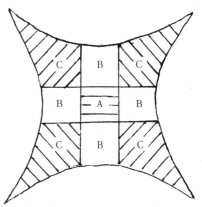

Fig. B. *Sew the pieces together in rows, then sew the rows together.*

Sewing Circle

Method: Bars cut from strip-pieced material.
Finished Block Size: 12″.

This traditional design from *Hearth and Home* magazine can be adapted to strip-piecing by cutting the center bars from strip-pieced material.

For the bars (piece D), sew long strips together to make strip-pieced material 6½″ high. Cut 2″-wide bars as in *Fig. A*—four bars for each block.

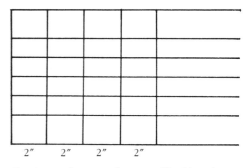

Fig. A. *For the center bars, cut 2″-wide strips from strip-pieced material.*

Trace individual patterns for pieces A, B and C, adding ¼″ seam allowances around; the arrows indicate the straight grain of the fabric. Cut templates from lightweight cardboard or plastic. For each block, cut eight A triangles from dark fabric, eight B and eight B reversed triangles from light fabric and 16 C triangles from medium fabric.

Sew the short side of a B triangle to a long side of an A triangle; sew a B reversed triangle to the other side of the A piece. Sew C triangles to each end to make a rectangle *(Fig. B)*. Repeat with the remaining pieces. Sew a rectangle to each side of a strip-pieced bar, having the A points to the outside (see pattern). Sew the resulting squares together,

alternating the direction of the center bars as in the photograph.

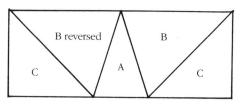

Fig. B. *Sew the A, B and C triangles together to form a rectangle.*

Pattern for Sewing Circle. Add ¼″ seam allowance around all pieces.

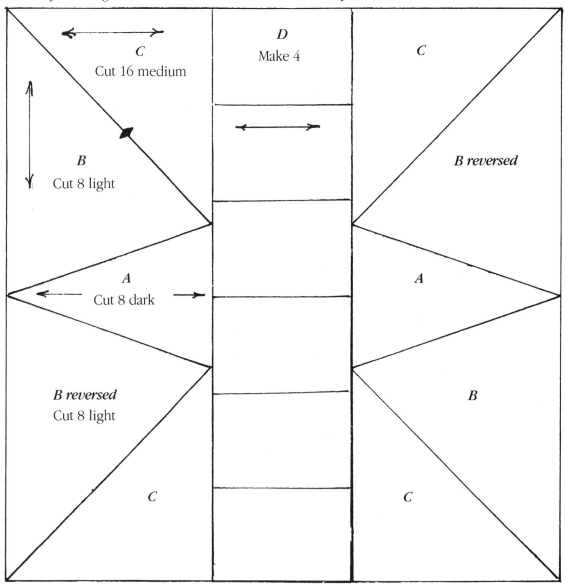

V.

Method 3: Combination Strip-Piecing

THE DESIGNS IN THIS GROUP ARE MADE BY SEWING LONG STRIPS OF fabric together in groups of two, three, four, five or even six strips, making a wider pieced strip. Cuts can be made straight across the seams of this wider strip to form squares and bands of color; or the cuts can be made at an angle to make triangles. These blocks, bands and triangles are then resewn together in a specific arrangement to create a design. Many complicated-looking designs can be made very simply and quickly by this method. Machine sewing is recommended.

The cutting and resewing of the pieced strips is similar to Seminole strip-piecing, but here it is done on a larger scale for quilts. The strips average about 2″ in finished width for most designs, but other widths can be used. Specific measurements, including seam allowances, are given with each design in this chapter. You will find many other designs in this category in my first book, *Quilting with Strips and Strings* (Dover 0-486-24357-5). See London Stairs, Basket Weave, Rail Fence, Brickwork, Spools, Twilight, Right and Left, Windmill and Deco Echo.

Using the rotary cutter, cut strips across the folded fabric the width specified in each pattern. The strip width must include the seam allowances on both sides; they are included in all the patterns in this book. Place two strips with right sides together and stitch the long sides in a ¼″ seam. Use the presser foot on your sewing machine as a seam guide, or place a piece of tape on the machine, ¼″

away from the needle. Add other strips as specified in the pattern instructions, always using ¼″ seams *(Fig. 44)*. Now work at the ironing board, using the steam setting on the iron to press each combination strip. First press each seam flat as it is sewn to stretch and set the stitches *(Fig. 45)*. Readjust the combination strip each time to press each seam separately. Next, press all the seams to one side, preferably toward the darker fabrics. Now turn the combination strip over to the right side and press it thoroughly to remove any tucks and pleats at seams. The combination

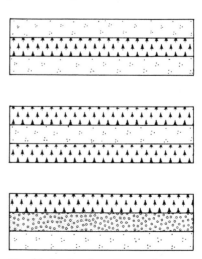

Fig. 44. *Sewing the strips together.*

strip fabric must be absolutely flat before making vertical and angled cuts. Since the cuts are made across the seams, cut only one combination strip at a time. I prefer to mark the strips with a pencil and ruler, then cut with the scissors for more accuracy across the thickness of the seams, but the rotary cutter can be used also to great advantage.

To cut squares from combination strips, the left edge of the pieced fabric must be perpendicular to the bottom edge, and will need trimming before any shapes can be cut. An easy way to accomplish this without a T-square or triangle is to lay a piece of typing paper over the combination strip, having the bottom edges lined up evenly. Since the paper is cut with a true right angle, the left edge can be used to mark the end *(Fig. 46)*. Mark with pencil and ruler and cut away any excess fabric.

"Squaring-off" is an easy way to cut squares from combination strips. Fold the left end of the fabric on the diagonal so that it is even with the top edge of the pieced strip; mark a vertical line along the right edge *(Fig. 47)*. With a ruler, check to see that the right edge measures the same distance as the top edge from the diagonal fold before cutting, so that the squares will be perfect. Sometimes the material may be distorted in pressing. In this case, squares cut by this method would not be perfect. The first square cut can be placed on the combination strip to mark other squares. Place the ruler on the edge of the square to mark a straight line.

Another way to obtain perfect squares is to make a cardboard square template, which should measure the *width* of the combination strip fabric on all four sides. Seam allowances will not have to be considered in either of these methods of cutting squares, since the strips included seam allowances.

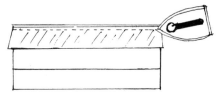

Fig. 45. *Press seams flat as sewn.*

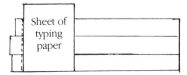

Fig. 46. *Make a straight edge on the left end of the fabric.*

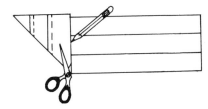

Fig. 47. *"Squaring-off" the strip.*

Lay the template on the combination strip fabric as shown for each design. Lay a ruler on the edge of the template and mark the fabric with a pencil. Cutting can be done with scissors or with the rotary cutter and guide. Cut only one combination strip at a time.

Reassemble the squares, bands or triangles as indicated in the instructions, taking ¼″ seams. Press seams flat as sewn, then to one side. Press the block on the right side to remove any tucks or pleats.

Blowing in the Wind

Method: Combination strips, cut first into squares, then into quarters to form triangles.

Finished Block Size: Approximately 10½″.

Number of Blocks for Wall Quilt: Nine—five dark and four light.

Setting: Three blocks across by three down.

Size of Quilt: Approximately 32″ × 32″ before borders, 40″ × 40″ including borders.

Materials for Wall Quilt
    45″-wide fabrics:
        1 yd. light print. Cut ten 2¾″-wide strips across the full width of the fabric for combination piecing. Cut four 1½″-wide strips across the full width of the fabric for inner borders.

        1½ yds. dark print. Cut ten 2¾″-wide strips across the full width of the fabric for combination piecing. Cut four 3½″-wide strips across the full width of the fabric for outer borders.
        1½ yds. lining fabric.
    Batting.

Using ¼″ seams, make five 10½″-wide combination strips, alternating the light and dark fabrics, as in *Fig. A*. With a steam iron, press the seams flat as sewn on both sides to set the stitches, then press the seams toward the dark fabric. Turn the strips to the right side and press again to remove any tucks or pleats.

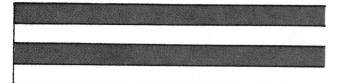

Fig. A. *Sew light and dark strips together to form combination strips.*

Fig. B. *"Square-off" the end of one combination strip.*

Fig. C. *Cut the squares diagonally to form triangles; number each triangle as shown.*

Wall quilt

Trim the left end of each combination strip at a right angle to the bottom edge, using a sheet of typing paper as a guide. Fold the left end of one strip on the diagonal to "square it off" as in *Fig. B*. Measure the horizontal and vertical edges to make sure they are the same and cut one 10½″ square. Cutting one layer of fabric at a time, use this square as a guide to cut 19 more squares. Four squares can be cut from each strip.

Mark and cut each square diagonally to make four triangles. Number each triangle on the wrong side as in *Fig. C;* stack like triangles together.

Sew triangles 1 and 2 together to make a square as in *Fig. D.* Repeat with remaining 1 and 2 triangles. Handling the units very carefully to avoid stretching the outer bias edges, sew four squares together as in *Fig. E* to complete a light block. Sew triangles 3 and 4 together in the same way *(Fig. F);* sew four squares together to complete a dark block *(Fig. G).*

Make four light and five dark blocks. Sew the blocks together, checkerboard fashion, in three rows of three blocks each. Sew the rows together. The dark blocks will be in the center and at the corners.

Sew the light border strips to the dark border strips in pairs. With the light strips on the inside, sew the borders to the quilt, mitering the corners. Place the quilt top over the batting and lining; quilt as desired. Bind the edges.

Fig. D. *Sew triangles 1 and 2 together to form a square.*

Fig. F. *Sew triangles 3 and 4 together.*

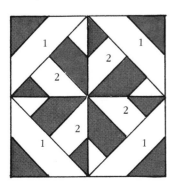

Fig. E. *Light block.*

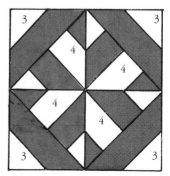

Fig. G. *Dark block.*

Repeating Crosses

Four-block setting

Method: Combination strips, cut into triangles.
Finished Block Size: 11″.
Number of Blocks for Quilt: 48.
Quilt Size: 66″ × 88″.
Setting: Six blocks across by eight blocks down.
Materials for Quilt
  Note: All strips are cut 2″ wide across the full width of the fabric.
  45″-wide fabrics:
    4¼ yds. light print or solid. Cut 70 strips.
    4¼ yds. dark print or solid. Cut 70 strips.
    6 yds. for lining.
  Batting.

Sew the light and dark strips together in pairs, using ¼″ seams. With a steam iron, press the seams flat as sewn on both sides to set the stitches, then press them toward the dark fabric. Press the strips again on the right side to remove any tucks.

Each block is made up of 16 matched triangles. Trace the pattern for the triangle, including the seam allowances, and cut a template from lightweight cardboard or plastic. Place half of the strips with the dark strip up and trace the template to the strips as in *Fig. A,* matching the line on the pattern to the seamline of the strips—six light triangles and five dark triangles. Place the remaining strips with the light strip up and trace the template to the strip as in *Fig. B*—six dark triangles and five light triangles. Cutting one strip at a time, cut a total of 384 light and 384 dark triangles. Stack like triangles together.

Using ¼″ seams, stitch two light triangles together along a short edge to form a larger triangle *(Fig. C)*. Repeat with two dark triangles *(Fig. D)*. Carefully matching the seamlines, sew the two larger triangles together along the long diagonal edges to form a square *(Fig. E)*. Make four squares for each block and sew them together with the dark triangles toward the center of the block. Make a total of 48 blocks.

Matching the seamlines, sew the blocks together in eight rows of six blocks each; sew the rows together. Light crosses will be formed at the intersections of the blocks. Place the quilt top over the batting and lining and quilt as desired. Bind the edges.

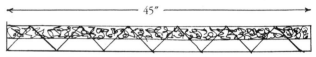

Fig. A. *Cut six light and five dark triangles.*

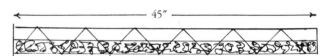

Fig. B. *Cut six dark and five light triangles.*

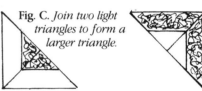

Fig. C. *Join two light triangles to form a larger triangle.*

Fig. D. *Join two dark triangles to form a larger triangle.*

Fig. E. *Sew the larger triangles together to form a square.*

Four-Block Wall Hanging

Cut five 2″-wide strips of each fabric to make five combination strips. Cut 32 light and 32 dark triangles. Construct four 11″ square blocks. Sew the blocks together in two rows of two blocks each. Sew the rows together. If desired, the wall hanging can be enlarged by adding borders of a contrasting fabric. Place the quilt top over the batting and lining; quilt as desired. Bind the edges.

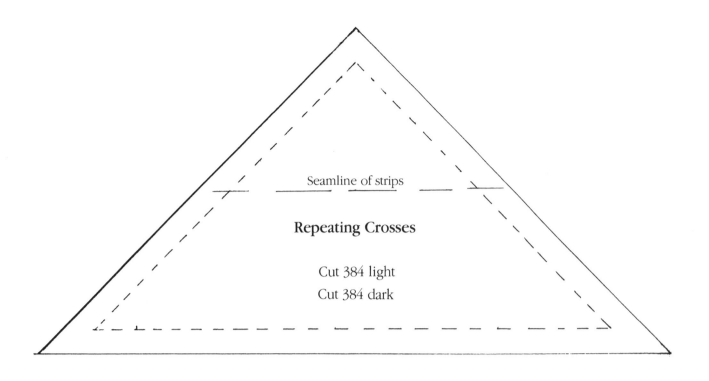

Seamline of strips

Repeating Crosses

Cut 384 light

Cut 384 dark

The Wishing Ring

Method: Combination strip-piecing.

Finished Block Size: 10″.

Number of Blocks for Large Wall Hanging: 25—12 strip-pieced and 13 dark.

Size of Large Wall Hanging: 50″ × 50″.

Number of Blocks for Small Wall Hanging: Nine—four strip-pieced and five dark.

Size of Small Wall Hanging: 30″ × 30″.

Note: For a balanced setting of this design, an odd number of blocks must be used both across and down.

Materials for Large Wall Hanging:

Note: Yardage has been calculated for the 25-block wall hanging, using the rotary cutter to cut the strips and pieces A and C from strips. See "Quick Cutting from Strips," page 6. All of the strips listed below are cut 1½″ wide across the full width of the fabric.

45″-wide fabrics:

½ yd. medium yellow print for strip #1. Cut ten strips.

½ yd. solid green for strip #2. Cut ten strips.

2 yds. navy/green/orange print for strip #3 and piece D. For strip #3, cut ten strips. Cut 13 D pieces.

¾ yd. light yellow print for A center squares and C triangles. See cutting directions below.

½ yd. orange solid for C triangles. See cutting directions below.

3 yds. lining fabric.

Batting.

This is not a difficult design, yet it is extremely effective when the strip-pieced blocks are alternated with dark print blocks. Fewer strip-pieced blocks are required this way than if they are set side by side.

Nine-block hanging

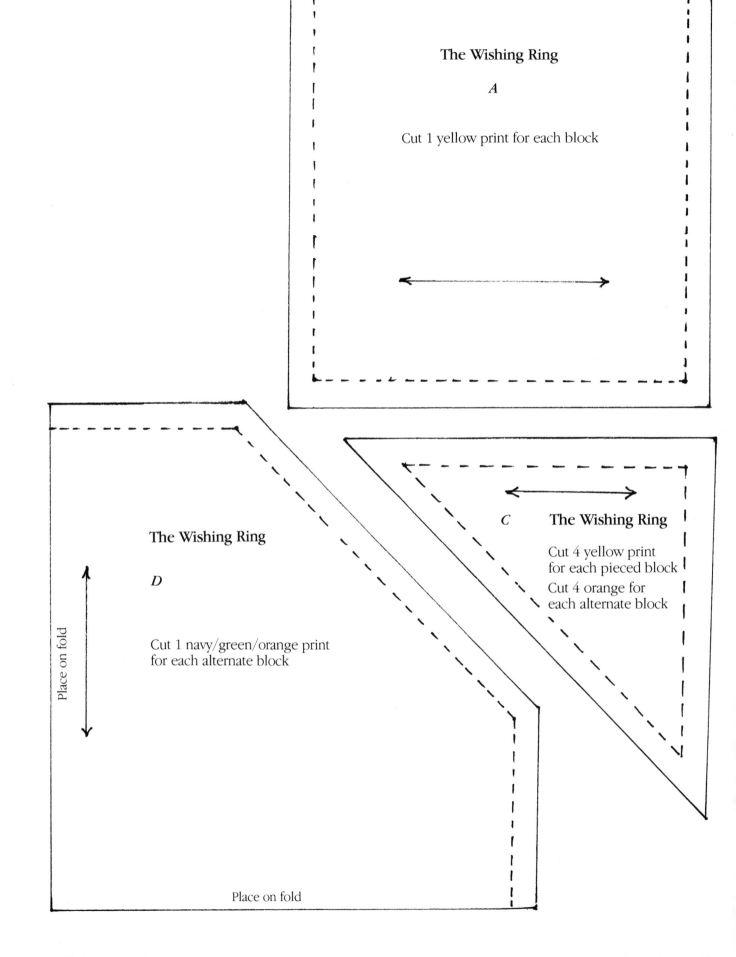

The Wishing Ring

A

Cut 1 yellow print for each block

The Wishing Ring

D

Cut 1 navy/green/orange print
for each alternate block

Place on fold

Place on fold

C **The Wishing Ring**

Cut 4 yellow print
for each pieced block

Cut 4 orange for
each alternate block

Trace the patterns for pieces A–D, including the seam allowance. To trace a full pattern for piece D, fold the paper into quarters and place the pattern on the folded edges. The arrows indicate the straight grain of the fabric. Cut templates from lightweight cardboard or plastic.

For A center squares, cut two 4½″-wide strips across the full width of the light yellow fabric. Trace the template to the strip and cut 12 squares. For C, cut three strips 4″ wide across the full width of the light yellow print and three strips from the orange solid fabric. Trace the templates to the strips as in *Fig. A* and cut 48 yellow triangles and 52 orange triangles.

With strip #2 in the center, sew strips #1–3 together with ¼″ seams to make ten combination strips. Following *Fig. B*, trace five B pieces across each strip. Cutting one strip at a time, cut a total of 48 B pieces. Mark the seamlines on the wrong side of all pieces.

Placing the #1 strip on the inside, stitch a B piece to opposite sides of an A square, starting and stopping the stitching exactly on the seamline. Sew a B piece to each remaining edge. Carefully match the bias ends of the B pieces and sew from the inside corners to the outside edge. Press the block flat on both sides. Sew yellow C triangles to the corners *(Fig. C)*. Make a total of 12 blocks.

For the alternate dark blocks cut 13 D pieces from navy/green/orange print, placing three across the fabric width. Sew orange C triangles to the corners of the D pieces *(Fig. D)*. Press the seams toward the D piece. Make 13 blocks.

Sew the blocks together, alternating them in checkerboard fashion, in five rows of five blocks each. The top row should begin and end with a dark block. Place the quilt top over the batting and lining and quilt as desired. Bind the edges.

The small wall hanging is made in the same way, making three rows of three blocks each.

Fig. A. *Trace template C to a 4″-wide strip.*

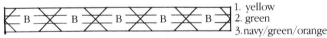

1. yellow
2. green
3. navy/green/orange

Fig. B. *Cut 48 B pieces from combination strips.*

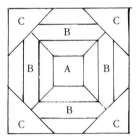

Fig. C. *Strip-pieced block.*

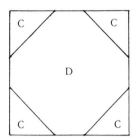

Fig. D. *Alternate dark block.*

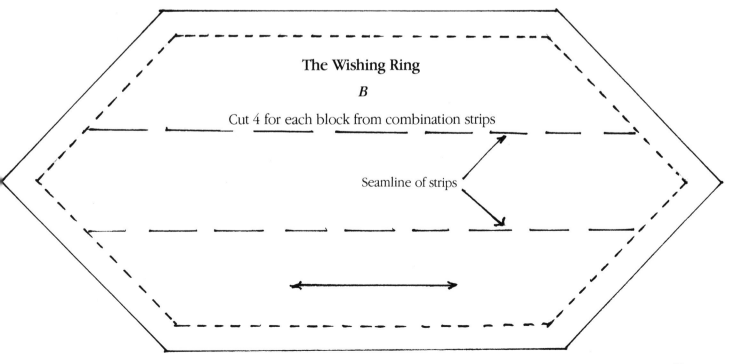

The Wishing Ring

B

Cut 4 for each block from combination strips

Seamline of strips

Economy or Windmill

Method: Combination strip-piecing.

Finished Block Size: 12″.

Number of Blocks for Quilt: 35—18 dark and 17 light.

Setting: Five blocks across and seven blocks down.

Quilt Size: 60″ × 84″ before borders; 72″ × 90″ including borders.

Materials for Quilt

Note: Strips listed below are cut 2½″ wide across the full width of the fabric.

45″-wide fabrics:

1 yd. dark print. Cut 12 strips.

1 yd. light print. Cut 12 strips.

1 yd. harmonizing solid. Cut 12 strips.

2⅓ yds. larger scale print for unpieced triangles. See cutting directions below.

2¾ yds. for borders.

5¼ yds. for lining.

Batting.

Four-block setting

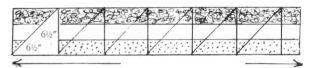

Fig. A. *Cut triangles from combination strips.*

Trace the pattern for the triangle including the seam allowance. Cut a template from lightweight cardboard or plastic.

With the solid fabric in the center, sew the dark print, light print and solid strips together with ¼″ seams to form 12 combination strips. Following *Fig. A,* trace the template to the strip, matching the lines on the template to the seams of the strip and being careful to draw all the diagonal lines in the same direction. Two different triangles will be formed *(Fig. B).* Cutting one strip at a time, cut six light and six dark triangles from each strip. Stack like triangles together.

Cut 12 strips 6½″ wide across the full width of the larger scale print fabric. Trace the template 12 times across one strip. Stack four strips with the marked strip on top and cut out the pieces with the rotary cutter. Repeat to cut a total of 140 triangles.

Sew the pieced triangles to the plain triangles along the diagonal edges to form squares *(Fig. C).* Sew four dark squares together so that the light points meet at the center *(Fig. D).* Sew four light squares together so that the dark points meet *(Fig. E).* Make 18 dark and 17 light blocks.

Sew the blocks together, alternating them in checkerboard fashion, in seven rows of five blocks each, carefully matching all seamlines *(Fig. F).*

Cutting along the lengthwise grain of the fabric, cut two border strips 3″ wide by 61″ long. Sew a strip to the top and bottom of the quilt. Cut side borders 6″ by 91″; sew to the sides. Place the quilt top over the batting and lining; quilt as desired. Bind the edges.

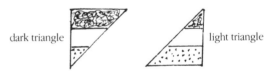

dark triangle / light triangle

Fig. B. *Two different triangles are cut from the combination strip.*

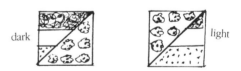

dark / light

Fig. C. *Sew the pieced triangles to the plain triangles to form squares.*

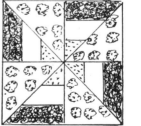

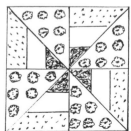

Fig. D. *Dark block.*   **Fig. E.** *Light block.*

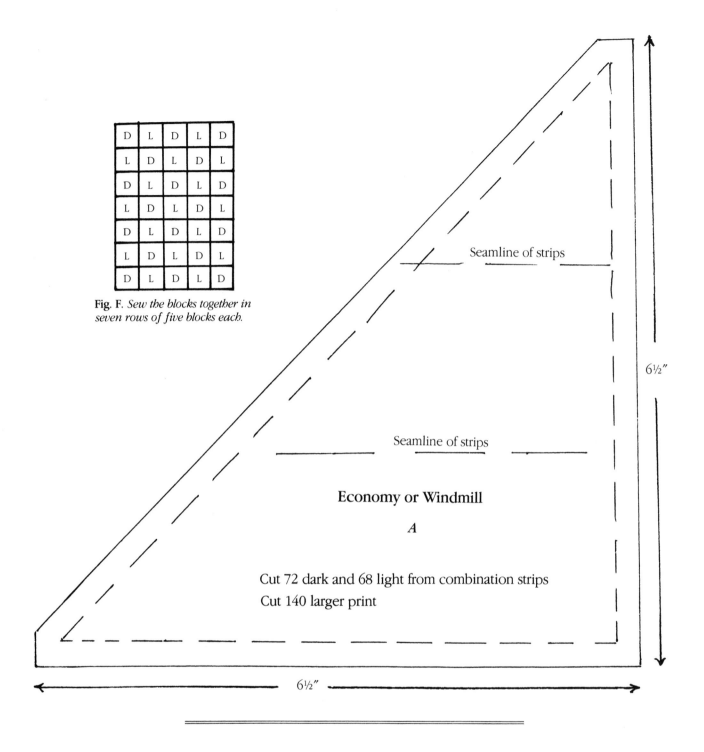

Fig. F. *Sew the blocks together in seven rows of five blocks each.*

Seamline of strips

Seamline of strips

Economy or Windmill

A

Cut 72 dark and 68 light from combination strips
Cut 140 larger print

6½″

6½″

Prosperity Quilt

Method: Combination strip-piecing.

Finished Block Size: 8″ × 10″.

Number of Blocks for Quilt: 72—36 dark blocks and 36 light blocks.

Setting: Six blocks across with 2″-wide dividing strips between the blocks; 12 blocks down with no dividing strips.

Quilt Size: 70″ × 96″ without borders. 4″-wide borders may be added to enlarge the quilt to 78″ × 104″.

Materials for Quilt

45″-wide fabrics:

3¾ yds. dark print. See cutting directions below.

3¾ yds. light solid. See cutting directions below.

2¾ yds. border fabric (optional). Cutting along the lengthwise grain, cut two side strips 4½″ by 98″ and two end strips 4½″ by 80″.

6½ yds. lining fabric for quilt with border.

Batting.

This old design, made of only two fabrics, suggests skyscrapers. The blocks are rectangular. The allover design is created by alternating rows of the dark and light blocks. The rows are mirror images of one another. The blocks across are separated by dividing strips, but no strips separate the rows. Instead of individually cutting and piecing small rectangles together, instructions are given for quick strip-piecing and cutting. Use the rotary cutter, mat and cutting guide to make this a very quick project.

Cut five dark strips 2½″ wide across the full width of the fabric (strip A). Cut five light strips 6½″ wide across the full width of the fabric (strip B). Sew the light and dark strips together in pairs to form five combination strips, then cut the strips into 2½″-wide strips *(Fig. A)*. Cut a total of 72 strips for the light blocks.

Cut five light strips 2½″ wide across the full width of the fabric (strip A). Cut five dark strips 6½″ wide across the full width of the fabric (strip B). Sew the light and dark strips together in pairs to form five combination strips, then cut the strips into 2½″-wide strips *(Fig. B)*. Cut a total of 72 strips for the dark blocks.

Cut nine strips each from the dark and light fabrics, cutting the strips 4½″ wide across the full width of the fabric (strip C). Sew the light and dark strips together in pairs to form nine combination strips. Cut each strip into 2½″-wide strips *(Fig. C)*. Cut a total of 144 strips. Half will be used for the light blocks and half for the dark blocks.

For the center D strips and the dividing D strips, cut strips 8½″ wide across the full width of the fabric (strip D). Cut four dark and four light strips. Cut each strip into 2½″-wide strips *(Fig. D)*. Cut a total of 66 light and 66 dark strips.

Prosperity Quilt—Four-block setting

Following *Figs. E* and *F,* sew the strips together with ¼″ seams to form 36 light and 36 dark blocks.

For the first and all odd-numbered rows, sew six dark blocks together along the short edges with light D strips between the blocks.

For the second and all even-numbered rows, sew six light blocks together with dark D strips between the blocks.

Sew the dark and light rows together in pairs, carefully matching the seams, so that the rows are mirror images of one another *(Fig. G)*. Sew the six pairs together.

If desired, sew border strips to the sides, then the top and bottom, of the quilt. Place the quilt top over the batting and lining; quilt as desired. Bind the edges.

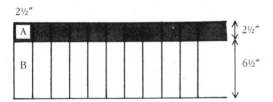

Fig. A. *Light A/B combination strip.*

Fig. B. *Dark A/B combination strip.*

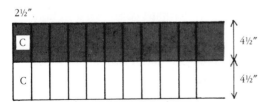

Fig. C. *C/C combination strip.*

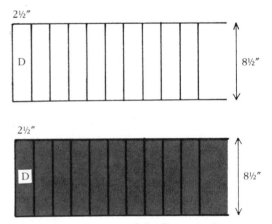

Fig. D. *Center strips and dividing strips D.*

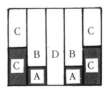

Fig. E. *Light block.*

Fig. F. *Dark block.*

66

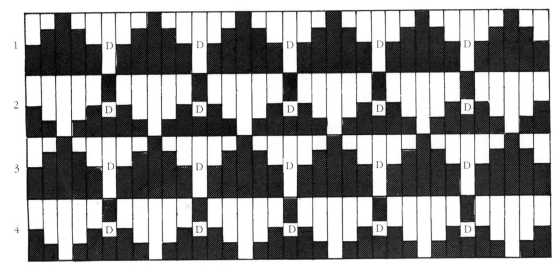

Fig. G. *The rows should be mirror images of one another.*

Circle of Love

Number of Blocks for Quilt: 35.
Setting: Five blocks across by seven blocks down.
Quilt Size: 60″ × 84″ without borders.
Materials for Quilt
   45″-wide fabrics:
      1½ yds. medium solid for piece A. See cutting
        directions below.
      1½ yds. light solid for piece B. See cutting directions
        below.
      3 yds. dark print for pieces C and D. See cutting
        directions below.
      5 yds. for lining.
   Batting.
   Thread.
   Needles for hand sewing.

This pretty design, with its appropriate name and curved seams, lends itself to hand sewing. By using some quick-cutting methods and combination strip-piecing, if desired, the design can be put together quickly and can be classified as a strip-pieced design. Make it in 6″ units, then join four units to form a 12″ block. The straight seams in this design can be sewn by machine.

   Yardages and instructions are given for a 60″ × 84″ quilt. To make the wall hanging shown in the photograph, see the instructions at the end.

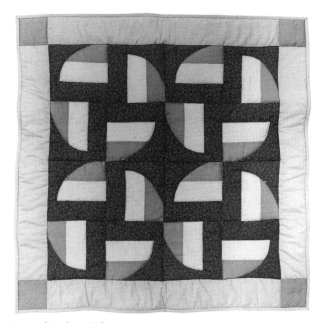

Four-block wall hanging

**Method 1: Quick-cutting the templates from strips with
   the rotary cutter.**
Trace patterns for pieces A, B, C and D, including the seam allowances. The arrows indicate the straight grain of the fabric. Cut templates from lightweight cardboard or plastic.

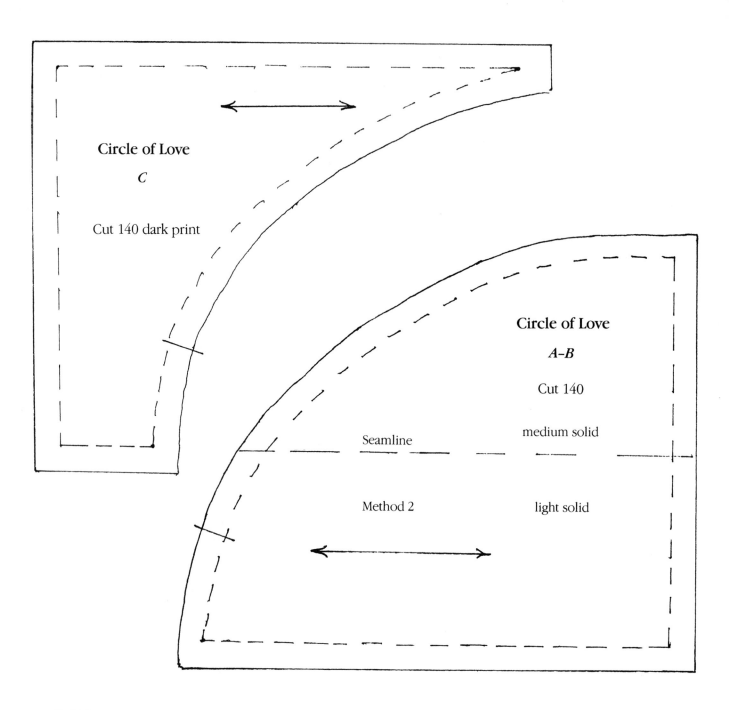

Circle of Love

C

Cut 140 dark print

Circle of Love

A–B

Cut 140

medium solid

Seamline

Method 2

light solid

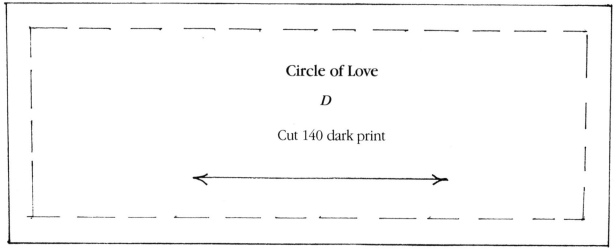

Circle of Love

D

Cut 140 dark print

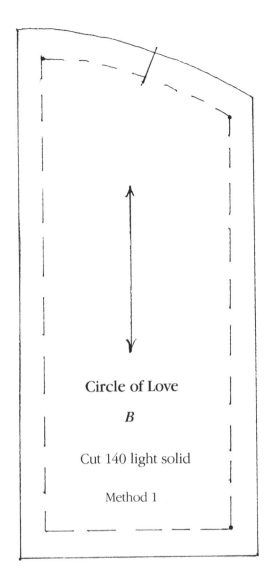

Circle of Love

B

Cut 140 light solid

Method 1

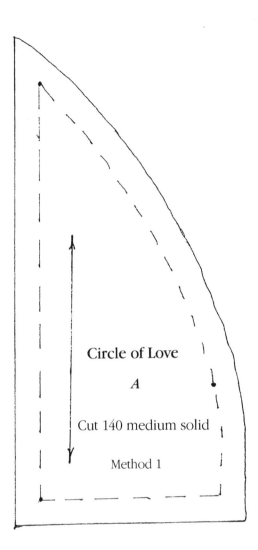

Circle of Love

A

Cut 140 medium solid

Method 1

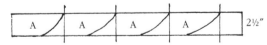

Fig. A. *Trace and cut the A pieces.*

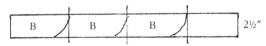

Fig. B. *Trace and cut the B pieces.*

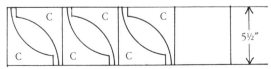

Fig. C. *Trace and cut the C pieces.*

Cut 18 strips 2½″ wide across the full width of the medium solid fabric. Trace template A to one strip as in *Fig. A.* Stack four strips with the right sides up and the marked strip on top; pin securely. Cut out the pieces. Cut a total of 140 A pieces.

Cut 18 strips 2½″ wide across the full width of the light solid fabric. Trace template B to one strip as in *Fig. B.* Stack four strips with the right sides up and the marked strip on top; pin securely. Cut out the pieces. Cut a total of 140 B pieces.

Cut ten strips 5½″ wide across the full width of the dark print. Trace and cut the C pieces following *Fig. C;* 14 C pieces can be cut from each strip. Cut a total of 140 C pieces.

Cut 21 strips 2½″ wide across the full width of the dark print fabric. Trace and cut the D pieces. Cut a total of 140 D pieces.

Sew A and B pieces together as in *Fig. D.* Pin a C piece to a joined A–B piece with the right sides together. Place the

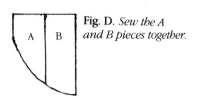

Fig. D. *Sew the A and B pieces together.*

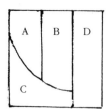

Fig. F. *Sew the D piece to the edge to form a square.*

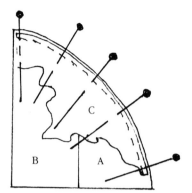

Fig. E. *Sew the C piece to the A–B piece by hand.*

Fig. G. *The completed block.*

wider end of the C piece even with the long straight edge of the B piece and match the notches on the curved edges. Place the pins about ½″ apart. The end of the C piece does not come all the way to the end of the A piece *(Fig. E).* Join the curved edges in a ¼″ seam by hand, clipping the seam allowance as needed. Press the seam toward the C piece. Sew the D pieces to the edge of the unit to form a 6½″ square *(Fig. F).*

Sew four squares together as in *Fig. G* to form a 12½″ block. The four D sections will form a pinwheel at the center of the block. Make 35 blocks.

Method 2: Combination strip-piecing.
Trace patterns for the joined A–B piece and for the C and D pieces, including the seam allowances. Cut templates from lightweight cardboard or plastic.

Cutting across the full width of the fabric, cut 18 strips 2½″ wide from the medium fabric and 18 strips 2½″ wide from the light fabric. Sew the medium and light strips together in pairs to form 18 combination strips.

Following *Fig. H,* trace the joined A–B template to each strip, placing the line on the template on the seam of the combination strip. Cut 140 pieces, cutting one layer of fabric at a time for accuracy.

Cut the C and D pieces and assemble the block as described above.

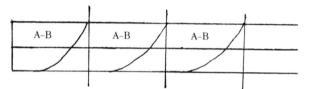

Fig. H. *Trace the A–B template to the combination strips.*

Sew the blocks together in seven rows of five blocks each. If desired, borders can be added to enlarge the quilt. Place the quilt top over the batting and lining. Quilt along the seamlines of the 6″ squares and along the curved edges of the A–B pieces. Bind the edges of the quilt.

Four-Block Wall Hanging

Make four blocks as described above. Sew the blocks together in two rows of two blocks each. From a harmonizing light fabric, cut four border strips 4½″ × 24½″. From medium fabric, cut four 4½″ corner squares. Sew a border strip to each side of the hanging. Sew a corner square to each end of each remaining border strip. Sew these strips to the top and bottom of the hanging. Place the quilt top over the batting and lining. Quilt along the seamlines of the 6″ squares and along the curved edges of the A–B pieces. Bind the edges of the quilt.

Little Houses Wall Hanging

Method: Quick cutting of templates from strips and combination strip-piecing.

Finished Block Size: 6″.

Number of Blocks for Wall Hanging: 12.

Setting: Three blocks across by four blocks down, with sashing strips between the blocks.

Size of Hanging: Approximately 28″ × 36″, including borders.

Materials for Wall Hanging

45″-wide fabrics (see cutting directions below):

⅜ yd. light blue for sky pieces A, C, L and O.

⅛ yd. red for chimney B.

¼ yd. crosswise stripe for roof N.

¼ yd. light print #1 for front of house, pieces D, F and M.

¼ yd. light print #2 for side of house, pieces G, I and J.

¼ yd. green print for grass K.

⅛ yd. bright yellow solid for door E and window H.

1¼ yds. contrasting fabric for sashing and border.

1⅛ yds. lining fabric.

30″ × 36″ piece of batting.

This popular pattern has a great many different pieces and, at first glance, seems rather complicated. However, the rotary cutter makes short work of cutting the pieces. Each block will be constructed in four horizontal rows. Use ¼″ seams throughout and press all the seams to one side as you work.

Trace the patterns for the sky O, house front M and roof N from the full-size block diagram. Add ¼″ seam allowances around each piece and cut templates from lightweight cardboard or plastic. The seam allowances are included in the dimensions given for the remaining pieces. Refer to the materials list for the fabrics to cut for each piece.

Row 1—Grass

Cut two strips 2″ wide across the full width of the fabric for the grass K. Cut across the strips vertically to form 12 strips 6½″ long.

Row 2—Front and Sides of House

Cut one 1½″-wide strip each for pieces D, E, F and G. Sew the strips together in order. Cut across the strip vertically to form 2″-wide strips *(Fig. A)*. Cut a total of 12 strips. Turn the strips so that the house end D is at the left *(Fig. B)*.

Cut one 1¼″-wide strip each for the window H and the

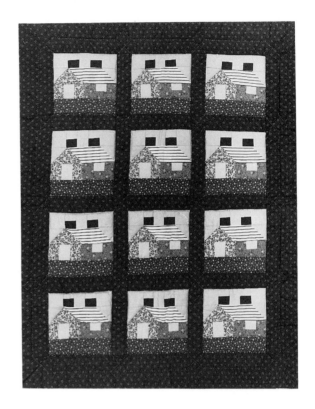

	2″	2″	2″	2″	2″	2″	
1½″	G	G	G	G	G	G	light print #2
1½″	F	F	F	F	F	F	light print #1
1½″	E	E	E	E	E	E	yellow
1½″	D	D	D	D	D	D	light print #1

Fig. A. *Cut strips for Row 1.*

Fig. B.

	1½″	1½″	1½″	1½″	
1¼″	H	H	H	H	yellow
1¼″	I	I	I	I	light print #2

Fig. C. *Cut strips for the window H and the house side I.*

Fig. D. *Row 2.*

house side I; sew the strips together. Cut the strip vertically to form 1½″-wide pieces *(Fig. C)*. Cut a total of 12 pieces.

Cut a strip 1½″ wide for house side J. Cut the strip vertically into 2″-wide pieces. Cut a total of 12 pieces.

Sew the pieces for Row 2 together, following *Fig. D*.

71

Row 3—Roof and Sky

Cut a 2⅛″-wide strip for the gable M. Following *Fig. E,* trace the template to the strip 12 times; cut out the pieces.

Cut two 2″-wide strips for the roof N from striped fabric. Following *Fig. F,* trace the template to the strip 12 times. The arrow on the template should be parallel to the stripes. Cut out the pieces.

Cut a 2½″-wide strip for the sky O. Following *Fig. G,* trace the template to the strip 24 times. Cut out the pieces.

Sew the pieces for Row 3 together following *Fig. H.* Handle the bias edges carefully to prevent their stretching and check to make sure that the corners are square before continuing.

Fig. E. *Cut piece M from a 2⅛″ wide strip.*

Fig. G. *Cut the sky O from a 2½″ wide strip.*

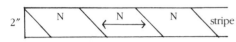

Fig. F. *Cut the roof N from a 2″ wide strip.*

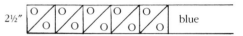

Fig. H. *Row 3.*

Block Diagram

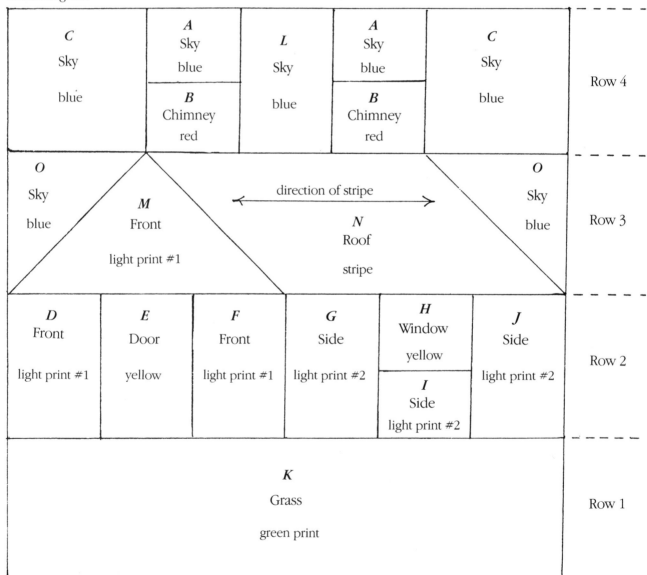

72

Row 4—Sky and Chimney

A little more than one strip will be required to cut 24 C pieces. Cut 2″-wide strips and cut them vertically to form 2″-wide squares.

A little more than one strip will be required to cut 24 A–B pieces. Cut the strips 1¼″ wide and sew them together. Cut the combination strip vertically to form 1½″-wide pieces *(Fig. I)*.

Cut a 1½″-wide strip for the sky L and cut it vertically to form 2″-wide pieces. Cut 12 pieces.

Sew the pieces for Row 4 together following *Fig. J*.

Sew the rows together following the block diagram, carefully matching the seams. Make 12 blocks.

Cutting along the lengthwise grain of the border and sashing fabric, cut three strips 2″ wide by 45″ long. From these strips, cut two sashing strips 30″ long and nine sashing strips 6½″ long.

Join four house blocks vertically, with a short sashing strip between each block *(Fig. K)*. Repeat to form three rows. Join the rows with the long sashing strips between *(Fig. L)*.

Cutting along the lengthwise grain of the fabric, cut two side borders 4″ by 38″ and two end borders 4″ by 30″. Sew the borders to the quilt, mitering the corners. Place the quilt top over the batting and lining. Quilt around each block and along the inside edge of the border. Bind the edges.

	1½″	1½″	1½″	1½″	1½″	1½″	
1¼″	A	A	A	A	A	A	blue
1¼″	B	B	B	B	B	B	red

Fig. I. *Cut the A–B pieces from a combination strip.*

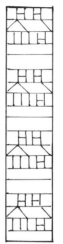

Fig. J. *Row 4.*

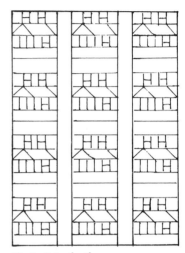

Fig. K. *Join three blocks to form a vertical row.*

Fig. L. *Join the three rows.*

VI.

Method 4:
Strip Designs Sewn in a Sequence Around a Central Shape

STRIP DESIGNS IN THIS GROUP ARE RELATED TO THE LOG CABIN BLOCK, because they begin with a central shape, such as a square, triangle, rectangle, diamond or hexagon, and the strips are added in a numerical sequence.

The variety of designs in this category seems endless because the designs can be changed so many different ways. Add to this the many, many settings of the Log Cabin blocks alone, and the number becomes staggering.

Log Cabin designs can be changed by changing the shape of the center, the order in which the strips are placed, the placement of the center shape within the blocks, the width of the strips and the placement of the colors.

Ways to Vary Log Cabin Designs and Sequence Sewing

1. Various Central Shapes

Square with strips the same width. ▢

Large square with narrow strips.

Rectangle, placed vertically or horizontally.

Triangle. △

Hexagon. ⬡

Diamond. ◇

Long hexagon. ⬡

Long diamond. ◇

2. Various Sequences for Attaching Strips

a. Turning the block one-quarter turn to add the next strip.

Typical Log Cabin—small square.

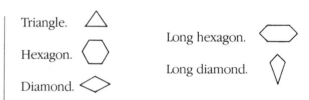

Log Cabin—large square.

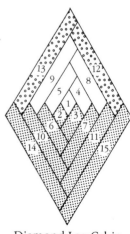

Diamond Log Cabin.

74

b. Turning the block one-third turn to add the next strip.

Triangle in the center.

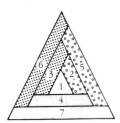

Large centered triangle with narrow strips.

c. Sewing strips in pairs to opposite sides of the central shape.

Courthouse Steps.

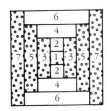

Rectangular Log Cabin (see page 79).

Hung center square. Use a base block and make each quarter of the block a different color.

d. Hexagon sequence—strips attached to opposite sides of a six-sided center.

Color Wheel Log Cabin— each side a different color (see page 84).

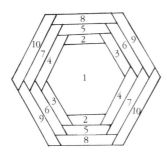

Long hexagon center.

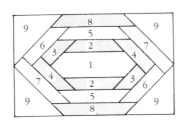

Hexagon Log Cabin.

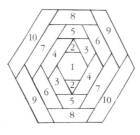

Long hexagon center. Set four squares together.

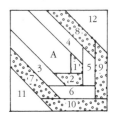

e. Pineapple sequence—four strips sewn in a round to center square, then four strips sewn at an angle across the corners, making eight color sections.

Pineapple (see page 81).

Maltese Cross.

Wild Goose Chase. The dark triangles are even numbers and are the same size.

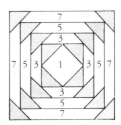

3. Different Placement of the Central Shape

a. Hung center—square turned diagonally. Courthouse Steps construction.

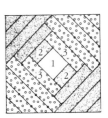

b. Square in the corner.

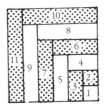

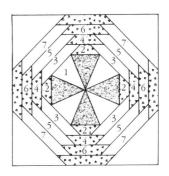

c. Square center on one edge. See Woodland Trees (page 78).

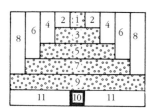

e. Off-center square; strips of two widths, creating a curved effect.

f. Diamond in one angle.

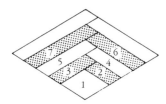

d. Triangle on one edge. See Silent Night (page 30).

g. Rocky Road to Kansas (see page 36).

4. Varying the Width of the Strips

a. Martha Washington's Log Cabin. Narrow strips with a large central square.

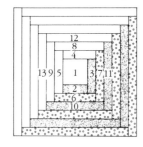

b. Thick and Thin. Each pair of strips increases in width.

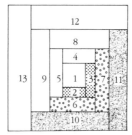

Early Log Cabin quilts were made with small blocks, about 6″ to 10″ square, and used ribbons or very narrow strips that finished about ½″ wide.

Strips that finish about 1½″ wide are a good average for today's larger blocks, which measure 9″ to 15″ square.

The smaller the strips, the more rounds are needed to fill out the block. There is no rule dictating how many strips to use around the central shape, except that each side should have the same number of strips.

5. Changing the Block with Color Placement

The traditional Log Cabin Block has a red central square symbolic of the hearth of the home. Sometimes yellow was used, representing the light in the window. If you want to change this for a particular color scheme, then do so without a second thought.

Your choice of colors for Log Cabin blocks will have a definite effect on the overall setting of the quilt. There must be great contrast between the light and dark fabrics in each block, or the design is lost. Many of the Log Cabin designs could be made in just two contrasting colors. Note that some blocks are light and dark on the diagonal, others are light and dark on opposite sides and still others have bands of color. Many interesting things happen when various prints with light backgrounds are used for the light side of the blocks. These may be different pastels, or all the same color background. Dark prints of saturated colors for the other half of the block will give great contrast.

Some of the designs with large central pieces will work nicely with a large print centered in the central shape. Other designs have strips all of one color on a side or corner. Study the diagrams for color placement and decide if you will use prints or solids, or a combination of both. Keep in mind that when blocks are set together without stripping, you will sometimes be matching light sides to light sides and sometimes light to dark or dark to dark.

a. Courthouse Steps.

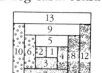

b. Typical Log Cabin construction.

c. Typical Log Cabin construction.

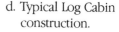

d. Typical Log Cabin construction.

e. Large diamond center.

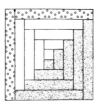

f. Square in the corner of the block. The squares are turned two ways in each row across.

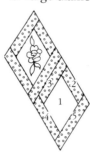

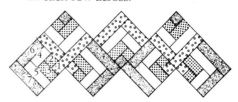

76

6. *Variation in Constructing the Block*

The typical Log Cabin construction is the sew, turn, press and cut method, where strips with straight ends are oversewn across ends of other strips, just as logs are stacked and assembled for a real log house.

In designs with central shapes that do not have right angles, the strip ends are angled when other strips are oversewn across them. You can see this in the hexagon, pineapple and triangular designs. These designs are more successful when pieced with strips cut with templates with the correct angles on the ends, so that the sides of the block will all measure the same. You will find complete instructions in this chapter for several of these designs. You can also draw your own full-size pattern on a large sheet of paper, beginning with the central shape in the size you want, then drawing the strips in the proper numerical order. This pattern will fit together like a jigsaw puzzle and will not include seam allowances. Be sure to add the seam allowances before you cut the strips and the center.

a. No-Template Method

The strips are cut to the desired width, including the seam allowances, sewn to the central shape in a ¼″ seam, turned to the right side, finger-pressed and cut to length after sewing. The length is determined by the strip (or central shape) just underneath the strip. You will have to gauge all seams by eye in this hand-sewn method.

b. Piecing the Block Over a Base

Paper. Use newsprint cut about the size of the finished block. Paper is ideal for machine sewing and can be torn away easily after the block is completed, and before joining other blocks. Baste the central shape to the paper, then add the strips in numerical order, taking ¼″ seams.

Fabric. A washed, thin muslin is ideal for the bases of the block, whether you are hand sewing or machine sewing. Cut it a little larger than the block, then trim it after all the strips are in place. Remember that you will be quilting through these layers, so keep the base fabric thin.

Interfacing. There is a very thin interfacing, called Trace-A-Pattern, that makes an ideal base for blocks for either hand sewing or machine sewing. Baste the central shape to the interfacing and add the strips in numerical order. The interfacing is not removed before sewing the blocks together.

c. Piecing Over Batting and Lining for Quilt-As-You-Go Blocks

Cut the batting the finished size of the block. Cut the lining square ¼″ larger on all sides than the finished block. Baste the central shape in place through all layers, and add the strips in numerical order. For both machine sewing and hand sewing, begin and end the stitching ¼″ in from the end of the strips so that the stitching lines will not cross on the underside. When machine stitching, pull the thread

ends to the top and clip them about ½″ away from the fabric. The ends will be caught when the next strip is added and the work will not have threads on the back. When stitching the last strip in place, where seams come to the outside edge of the block, begin and end the stitching about 1″ away from the strip ends. Sew this 1″ by hand in the top layers only. This leaves ample room for joining the blocks.

Refer to page 87 for assembling the quilted blocks.

Log Cabin Hybrids

Each square in the following diagrams represents a typical Log Cabin block, divided diagonally into light and dark halves.

Typical Log Cabin block.

Ribbons or Pinwheels.

Light and Dark.

Variation on Barn Raising.

Variable Star.

Zigzag.

Windblown.

Carpenter's Wheel. There are four different blocks—one solid and three Log Cabin.

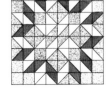

77

Woodland Trees, Log Cabin Source

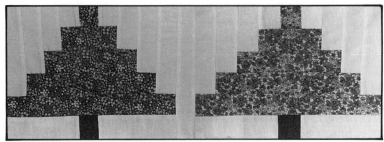

Two blocks

Method: Strips sewn in Log Cabin sequence to a rectangular base. This design can also be pieced without a base.

Finished Block Size: 9″ × 13″.

Number of Blocks for Quilt: 41 whole blocks, eight half blocks.

Setting: Five blocks across and nine blocks down.

Quilt Size: 70″ × 81″ without borders.

Materials for Quilt

All of the trees in the quilt may be made of the same green flowery print, or each tree can be made of a different green print to represent spring colors. You can also use tan, russet, brown and gold for fall colors. The strips around the trees represent the sky, so choose a sky-blue solid. Use solid brown for the tree trunks.

45″-wide fabrics, for 45 blocks (cut all strips 2″ wide across the full width of the fabric):

3 yds. green print. Cut 47 strips.

4 yds. solid sky blue. Cut 67 strips. This includes the 39 joining strips (piece #17).

⅓ yd. solid brown. Cut four strips. Cut the strips vertically to form 2″ squares for the tree trunks (piece #14). Cut a total of 45 squares.

For one block (if blocks are to be different fabrics), you will need one 2″-wide strip of print, two 2″-wide strips (or 2″ × 58″) of sky blue and a 2″ square of brown for the tree trunk #14.

Newspaper or 6 yds. 36″-wide very thin interfacing for bases.

5 yds. for lining.

Batting.

Cut 9½″ × 15½″ bases for 45 blocks. Both the blocks and the joining strips will be attached to the bases. On each base, measure 6¾″ from the left edge to mark the center of the block and the placement of piece #1 *(Fig. A)*. To form bases for the half-blocks, cut along this center line.

For each block, cut two 2″ squares of blue (pieces #1 and 3) and one 2″ square of print (piece #1) from the strips. Also cut two strips of blue 2″ by 7″ for pieces #15 and 16. The remaining strips will not be cut to length until after they are attached to the base.

Sew pieces #1, 2 and 3 together with #1 in the center. Pin this strip to the top edge of the base, centering it over the

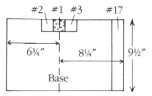

Fig. A. *Mark the center of the block.*

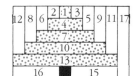

Fig. B. *Sew a print strip to the bottom of the first strip.*

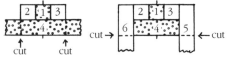

Fig. C. *Add a blue strip to each side.*

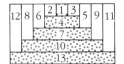

Fig. D. *Add the strips in numerical order.*

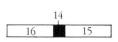

Fig. E. *Join pieces #14, 15 and 16.*

Fig. F. *Sew a blue strip to the right-hand edge of the block.*

Fig. G. *Half-block for left edge.*

Fig. H. *Half-block for right edge.*

line marked on the base. Sew a print strip across the bottom of this strip, then trim the ends even with the ends of the first strip *(Fig. B)*. See page 22 for sewing strips to a shaped base. Turn the print strip to the right side and pin through the seam. Sew a blue strip to each side *(Fig. C)*. Continue to add strips in numerical order to the bottom and sides of the block *(Fig. D)*. For the last strip, sew pieces #14, 15 and 16 together *(Fig. E)*. Sew this strip to the bottom of the block. Sew a blue joining strip to the right-hand edge of the block *(Fig. F)*. If paper was used for the base, tear it away carefully. Make 36 blocks like this. Make five more blocks, omitting the joining strip. Trim the right-hand edge of the base even with the edge of the block.

Construct four half-blocks as in *Fig. G* and four half-blocks as in *Fig. H*.

Fig. I. *Odd-numbered rows.*

Fig. J. *Even-numbered rows.*

The quilt is assembled in nine horizontal rows. For rows 1, 3, 5, 7 and 9, sew five blocks together as in *Fig. I.* Note that there are no joining strips on the right-hand end of the row. For rows 2, 4, 6 and 8, sew four whole blocks and two half blocks together as in *Fig. J.* Sew the rows together, carefully matching the seams.

If desired, borders may be added to enlarge the quilt. Place the quilt top over the batting and lining. Quilt along the seamlines of the strips or as desired. Bind the edges of the quilt.

Rectangular Courthouse Steps

Method: Log Cabin sequence, with a rectangular center.
Finished Block Size: 14″ × 20″.
Number of Blocks for Quilt: Seven B blocks, ten C blocks and six half B blocks.
Setting: Five blocks across by four blocks down. No sashing is used. The B and C blocks alternate.
Quilt Size: Approximately 78″ × 88″, including borders.
Materials for Quilt
 Note: The strips listed below are cut 2½″ wide across the full width of the fabric.
 45″-wide fabrics:
  ½ yd. light solid (fabric A). Cut five strips.
  2 yds. medium solid (fabric B). Cut 20 strips.
  2 yds. dark solid (fabric C). Cut 20 strips.
  1½ yds. coordinating light print (fabric D). Cut 15 strips.
  2½ yds. light print for borders. This can be the same fabric as D. Cutting along the lengthwise grain, cut four borders 4″ × 82″. The borders will be trimmed to the proper length after they are sewn on.
  5¾ yds. fabric for lining.
  Batting.

This simple Log Cabin block uses only four colors. Make a quilt alternating the placement of the colors in the blocks, or use a single block for a placemat. Instructions and materials are given here for a quilt using blocks with a 12″-long center *(Fig. A)*. To make the variation block shown in the photograph, see the instructions at the end.

Several different methods can be used to piece the blocks. The strips can be sewn with right sides together by hand or machine in the conventional manner; they can be sewn to a fabric or paper base, or they can be sewn by the quilt-as-you-go method to the batting and lining.

Patterns are given only for pieces #1 and 2. Trace these patterns, including the seam allowances. Cut templates from lightweight cardboard or plastic. The other strips will be sewn into place, then trimmed even with the strip

Variation Block

underneath. Use a ruler to make sure to cut the ends straight.

There are two different blocks, with the colors placed differently in each block *(Figs. B and C)*. Note that the light fabric (A) and the print fabric (D) are in the same position in all the blocks.

Following *Figs. B and C* for the colors, cut one #1 and two #2 pieces for each block. Sew the #2 pieces to the ends of the #1 piece. If you plan to sew the pieces to a base, mark

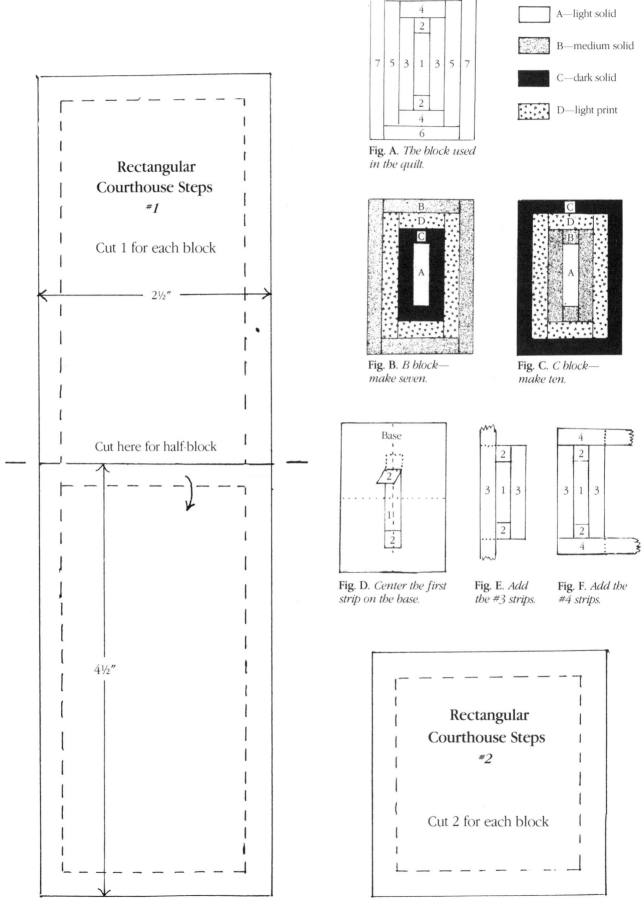

Rectangular
Courthouse Steps
#1

Cut 1 for each block

2½″

Cut here for half-block

4½″

Fig. A. *The block used in the quilt.*

☐ A—light solid

▨ B—medium solid

■ C—dark solid

▥ D—light print

Fig. B. *B block— make seven.*

Fig. C. *C block— make ten.*

Base

Fig. D. *Center the first strip on the base.*

Fig. E. *Add the #3 strips.*

Fig. F. *Add the #4 strips.*

Rectangular
Courthouse Steps
#2

Cut 2 for each block

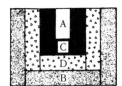

Fig. G. *Half-block.*

Row 1 Row 2 Row 3 Row 4 Row 5

B		B		B
	B		B	
C				C
	C		C	
B		B		B
	B		B	
C		C		C
	C		C	
B		B		B

Fig. H. *Sew the rows together.*

the horizontal and vertical center of the base. Center the #1 strip over these lines *(Fig. D)*. Sew #3 strips to the sides of the joined strip and trim the ends even with the #2 pieces *(Fig. E)*. Add #4 strips at the top and bottom *(Fig. F)*. Continue adding strips in numerical order (see *Fig. A*).

Make six half-blocks as in *Fig. G*, cutting the #1 strips 4½″ long.

The quilt is assembled in five vertical rows. For rows 1, 3 and 5, sew a C block to the top and bottom of a B block; sew half blocks to each end. For rows 2 and 4, sew two B and two C blocks together, alternating the blocks. Sew the rows together *(Fig. H)*. Sew borders to the sides, then to the top and bottom of the quilt.

Place the quilt top over the batting and lining (if you have not used the quilt-as-you-go method) and quilt as desired. Bind the edges of the quilt.

Variation Block

In this variation, the #2 pieces contrast with the #3 pieces, rather than matching them. If the #2 pieces are cut from fabric B, cut the #3 pieces from fabric C and vice versa. Cut the #1 piece 6″ long and the #2 pieces 5¾″ long.

Pineapple Log Cabin

Method: Strips sewn in Log Cabin sequence to sides and corners of a central square to make eight color sections over a square muslin base.

Finished Block Size: 15½″.

Number of Blocks for Quilt: 20.

Setting: Four blocks across by five blocks down without sashing so that an allover design is formed.

Quilt Size: 60″ × 75″ without borders.

Materials for Quilt

45″-wide fabrics (see cutting directions below):

4 yds. Permapress muslin.

4 yds. red/white print.

2½ yds. border fabric (optional).

5 yds. lining fabric.

5 yds. 36″-wide thin muslin for bases.

Batting.

Water-erasable marking pen.

Four-block setting

This beautiful design symbolizing hospitality has long been a favorite of quiltmakers, even though many may think its construction is complicated. In this instance, looks are deceiving, for when the secrets of the construction are revealed, the method is very simple. Even though the sequence sewing for the Pineapple is different from other Log Cabin designs because it has eight sides, you will find that with a little preparation and the cutting of a few pieces from templates, the design will be easy and symmetrical. The secret lies in the use of the rotary cutter for quick and easy cutting of the strips, quick machine sewing using the presser foot (or a line marked on the machine throat plate with tape) for gauging accurate ¼″ seams throughout, and the marking of a few guidelines on the fabric base square. Read through all of the instructions before you begin to become familiar with the process. As you sew, you will find that you will establish a "rhythm" to attaching the strips.

Wash and press all of the fabrics, especially the thin muslin used for the base squares, to shrink them, remove the sizing and to prevent the bleeding of the color.

Use the rotary cutter and the 1½″-wide cutting guide to cut light and dark strips across the fabric. This width includes the seam allowances.

Cutting Instructions for Each Block

Trace the patterns for the central square #1, central triangle #2 and the corner triangle #3, including the seam allowance. Cut templates from lightweight cardboard or plastic.

Cut a 17″ thin muslin square for the base. Cut one central square from Permapress muslin. Cut four central triangles #2 and four corner triangles #3 from the red print. Cutting across the full width of the fabric, cut four 1½″-wide strips each from the Permapress muslin and the red print.

Preparing the Base Squares

To locate the exact center of the base square, draw diagonal lines from corner to corner, using the water-erasable pen. Fold the block in half lengthwise and crosswise to find the horizontal and vertical center; draw in these lines. All of the lines should intersect in the center of the block.

To help you position the first few pieces, measure and mark 2⅞″ from the center along each diagonal line. Connect the marks to form a 4″ square in the center of the block with the edges parallel to the edges of the block. The muslin strips will be aligned with this square. Next, measure and mark 3⅞″ from the center along the horizontal and vertical lines. Connect the marks to form a 5½″ square set diagonally on the base. The red strips will be aligned with this diagonal square *(Fig. A)*.

Constructing the Block

Baste the central square to the base with the points on the horizontal and vertical lines. This square will be set diagonally on the base.

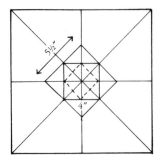

Fig. A. *Draw guidelines on the base square.*

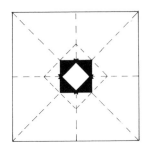

Fig. B. *The central square surrounded by the red central triangles.*

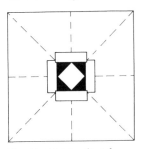

Fig. C. *Add the first four light strips.*

Fig. D. *Add four red strips.*

Fig. E. *The completed block.*

Pin two red #2 triangles to opposite sides of the central square with the right sides together and raw edges matching. Stitch in a ¼" seam, using the presser foot or a piece of tape placed on the machine bed ¼" away from the needle as a guide. Turn the strips to the right side and press. Add the remaining #2 triangles to the other sides of the square, stitching across the ends of the first triangles. When turned to the right side and pressed, these triangles should just fit within the 4" square marked on the base. You now have a square within a square (Fig. B).

Cut four 4"-long pieces from a long muslin strip. Pin two strips over opposite sides of the red triangles with right sides together and raw edges matching. Adjust the strips so that the seamline will just cross the points of the central square without cutting them off. Stitch and turn the strips to the right side. Press. Sew the other two strips in place, crossing the ends of the first strip (Fig. C).

Next you will add four red strips. Cut four pieces 3½" long from one of the long red strips. Center a strip across the ends of two of the light strips so that the edge of the red strip is on the 5½" square marked on the base. This strip must be parallel to the edges of the center square #1 in order to align the red strips that will be added later. Stitch in a ¼" seam. Repeat on the opposite side of the block; then sew red strips to the other two sides in the same manner (Fig. D). Lift the strips each time after sewing and cut away the little triangles on the ends of the strips underneath so that the darker fabric will not show through the light fabric. You now have the basic strips in place and have established the proper angles for the placement of the subsequent strips.

Note that each round of strips is added across the ends of the previous round of strips. Check your stitching each time to make sure that all of the strips in a round are the same width. Also make sure that the points of the central square and the points of the first red triangles are clearly defined. Since corrections cannot be made later, check your work carefully as you go and make any small adjustments before adding other strips.

Subsequent strips are not measured and cut before attaching; instead, a 45"-long strip is placed against the raw edges of a side with about ¼" extending on the left end, then stitched in a ¼" seam. Stitching will begin and end at the edges of the strip underneath. Trim the long strip straight across, ¼" beyond the end of the stitching. Turn the strips to the right side and press. Trim away the little triangles on the ends of the strips underneath each time before adding other strips.

Continue to add strips, four light strips in one round, then four red strips in the next round, until six light strips have been added. The light strips should come to the edges of the base square. If any of the base fabric shows, trim it away on four sides.

Continue adding red strips toward the four corners for a total of eight strips (beginning with the red central triangles). Sew a red #3 triangle to each corner (Fig. E). Turn and press.

Sew the blocks together in five rows of four blocks each. Turn the blocks so that they match and try to match up the light strips before sewing. Borders can be added if you want to enlarge the quilt. Place the quilt top over the batting and lining. Quilt along the seamlines of the pieces. Bind the edges of the quilt.

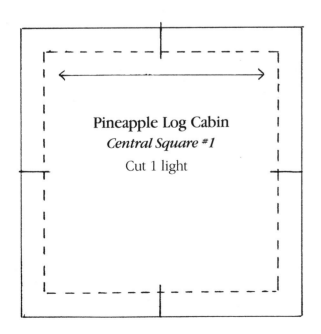

Pineapple Log Cabin
Central Square #1
Cut 1 light

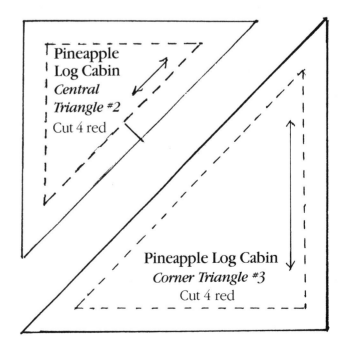

Pineapple Log Cabin
Central Triangle #2
Cut 4 red

Pineapple Log Cabin
Corner Triangle #3
Cut 4 red

Color Wheel Hexagon

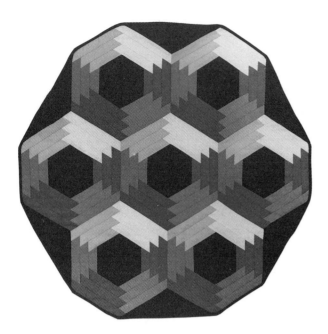

Wall Hanging

Method: Strips sewn to a paper base in Log Cabin sequence around a central hexagon.

Finished Block Size: 11″ side to side; 12¾″ point to point.

Number of Blocks for Wall Hanging: Seven.

Size of Wall Hanging: 32″ × 32″.

Materials for Wall Hanging

Note: Choose bright, pure colors to obtain a color-wheel effect. Cut all strips 1½″ wide across the full width of the fabric.

45″-wide fabrics:

¼ yd. solid red. Cut three strips.
¼ yd. solid green. Cut three strips.
¼ yd. solid blue. Cut three strips.
¼ yd. solid orange. Cut three strips.
¼ yd. solid purple. Cut three strips.
¼ yd. solid yellow. Cut three strips.
¾ yd. black.
1 yd. double-faced pre-quilted fabric for backing.
Newspaper for bases.

Trace patterns for central hexagon, fill-in triangle and strips #1–9, including the seam allowance. To make a full pattern for the fill-in triangle, trace the piece to the folded edge of the paper and cut it out. In order to save space, the patterns for the strips are combined in sets of three. Begin tracing each pattern at the bottom or the left-hand edge. Cut templates for all pieces from lightweight cardboard or plastic. Mark the strip number and the color on each template. Note that each template is used to cut pieces of two different colors.

Stack the red and green strips in groups of three. Trace the templates to the strips *(Fig. A)* and cut seven each of

strips #1, 4 and 7 from each color. Cut seven each of strips #3, 6 and 9 from purple and from yellow. Cut seven each of strips #2, 5 and 8 from blue and from orange. Placing the arrow on the template on the lengthwise grain of the fabric, cut seven central hexagons from black. Mark one edge for the top. Also cut six fill-in triangles and four yds. of 2″-wide bias binding from black.

Cut seven 14″ square bases from newspaper. These are used to stabilize the stitching and will be torn away before the blocks are joined. They do not have to be exactly 14″, but must be large enough to accommodate the block.

The strips are added two at a time in numerical order to opposite sides of the central hexagon. Each side of the hexagon will be a different color *(Fig. B)*.

Pin the central hexagon in the center of the paper base with the marked edge at the top. With right sides together, lay the wider edge of the green #1 strip along the top edge of the hexagon. On each end, a small ¼″ triangle will extend over the edges of the piece underneath. Stitch the pieces together in a ¼″ seam. The stitching will begin and end in the angles formed at each end of the pieces. Clip the threads closely on both ends. Lay the red #1 strip at the bottom of the central hexagon and stitch into place as before. Press these seams flat as sewn. Turn the strips to the right side and press again to remove any tucks. The ends of these strips will line up evenly with the sides of the central hexagon. The green strip will be used to align subsequent strips.

Next add the #2 strips of blue and orange. The blue strip is placed to the right of the green strip, and the orange strip is placed to the left of the red strip. The strips will be opposite one another. The #2 strips will be sewn across one end of the #1 strips and should be parallel to the edge of the hexagon underneath. Check the seamline where the strips are sewn over the ends of the strips underneath; do

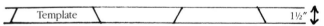

Fig. A. *Trace templates to strips. Strips of two colors may be stacked for cutting.*

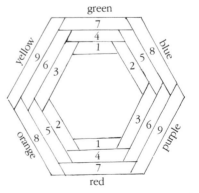

Fig. B. *Add the strips in numerical order.*

Fig. C. *Arrange the blocks in three vertical rows.*

not shorten the strip underneath when stitching the seam. Careful placement is necessary to keep the block true. If a strip is placed correctly, it should fit on the side with only a ¼″ triangle extending on each end. Stitch, then press the strip to the right side as before.

Next add the #3 strips of purple and yellow. The purple strip is placed between the red and blue; the yellow is placed between the orange and green. Check the placement, sew and press as before. These strips are sewn across two ends of the strips already in place and must be parallel to the edges of the hexagon, without shortening the ends of the strips underneath. Sew, then turn the strips to the right side and press.

Now all of the colors are properly placed. Subsequent strips will be matched in opposite pairs to the color of the first six strips. Start the second round with green #4, then add red #4. Add blue #5 and orange #5. Complete the second round with purple #6 and yellow #6.

Round three begins with green #7 and red #7. Add blue #8 and orange #8. Lastly, add purple #9 and yellow #9. Each side of the hexagon now has three strips of the same color on a side.

Make any adjustment to the strip width or the placement as you go, even if it means ripping out stitches. Do not shorten the strips underneath when stitching the strips across a side. Do not cut off the ends of the strips, just in case there are later adjustments.

Lay out all the pieced blocks with the green strips at the top *(Fig. C)*. The center vertical row will have three blocks, with red matching green at the bottom of the first hexagon. The two side rows will have two blocks, with red matched to green between the blocks. Join the blocks in rows, beginning and ending the stitching exactly on the seamline. It is important to leave a seam allowance for making the seams in the opposite direction.

Lay out the three rows and match the zigzag vertical seams. Sew one side of a block at a time in a ¼″ seam, starting at the inside angle, ¼″ away from the edge of the fabric. End the stitching at the outside edge, ¼″ away from the edge of the fabric. Tie off the threads at the angles and the ends of the seams. Press the seams open. There should be no puckers or holes at the intersection of the three seams.

Baste the fill-in triangles in place around the outside edges of the work. If the work does not lie flat, it may be necessary to take a wider seam on one side of the triangle, from the angle to the outside edge. When all of the triangles are basted, press the work and check again to see that the work is flat before machine stitching. Any overhang of the triangles can be trimmed later. Always start at the inside angle of the hexagon and sew to the outside edges. Trim away any dark points that may show through lighter fabrics on the top side.

Place the top over the pre-quilted backing to stabilize the work. Baste well and quilt as desired. Another way to attach the top to the backing is by "blind tacking." To do this, pin the work to the backing along the center seamline; then flip the bottom half of the work over the top and baste, catching the crosswise seams only. Do this along the seamlines at the top and bottom of the blocks and at the top and bottom of the black hexagons. Also tack the sides of the hexagons. Work on one half of the piece at a time, then turn the piece and do the other half of the tacking. Baste around the outside edges and machine-stitch ⅛″ from the edge.

Bind the edges of the quilt with the black bias binding.

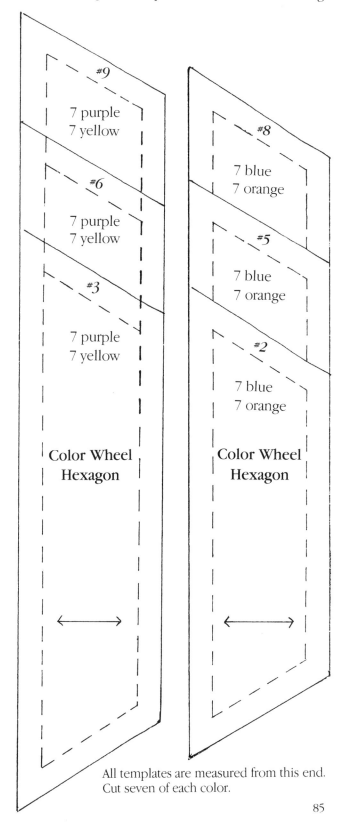

#9

7 purple
7 yellow

#8

7 blue
7 orange

#6

7 purple
7 yellow

#5

7 blue
7 orange

#3

7 purple
7 yellow

#2

7 blue
7 orange

Color Wheel
Hexagon

Color Wheel
Hexagon

All templates are measured from this end.
Cut seven of each color.

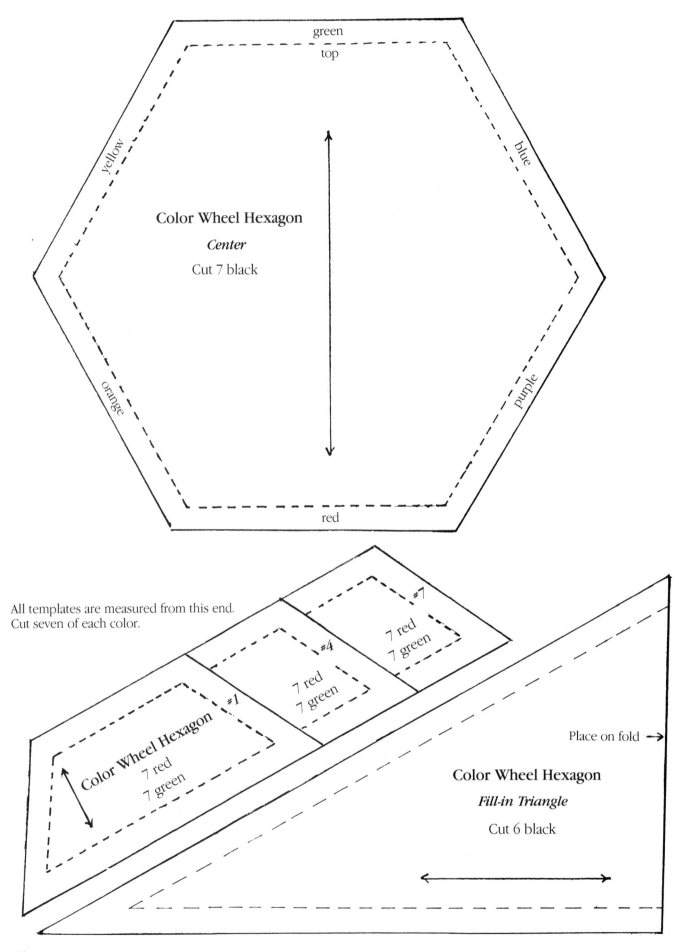

green

top

yellow

blue

Color Wheel Hexagon

Center

Cut 7 black

orange

purple

red

All templates are measured from this end.
Cut seven of each color.

#1

#4

#7

Color Wheel Hexagon

7 red
7 green

7 red
7 green

7 red
7 green

Place on fold →

Color Wheel Hexagon

Fill-in Triangle

Cut 6 black

VII.

Method 5: Quilt-As-You-Go Techniques

"QUILT-AS-YOU-GO," SOMETIMES REFERRED TO AS "LAP QUILTING," WAS thoroughly covered in my first book, *Quilting with Strips and Strings* (Dover 0-486-24357-5). Further help can be found in several of the books listed in "Suggested Reading," page 12.

Essentially this method involves quilting the top layer, batting and lining together, one block or section of a quilt at a time, before joining it to the rest of the quilt. The section may consist of a number of blocks joined across the width of the quilt, blocks joined vertically for the length of the quilt, or four blocks joined to form a larger piece, according to the setting plan of the quilt top. The sections might also include sashing strips on the sides of the blocks, and outside border strips.

When quilting the blocks or sections, at least ½″ must be left unquilted at the edges of each block so that the batting can be trimmed and the lining folded out of the way when the blocks are joined. Plan the quilting design so that it will be completely contained within the section, and quilt no closer than ½″ from the edges of the sections.

This method of quilt assembly has two major advantages: the work is portable and the quilting can be done with either a small frame or with no frame at all (hence the term "lap quilting"). However, it does require more stitching than conventional methods, since the edges of the sections must be overlapped on the back of the quilt and blind-stitched together by hand. The batting should be trimmed so that the edges butt together under this seam.

See "Hidden Seam Borders," on page 9, for adding a border to a quilt constructed by the quilt-as-you-go method.

Some strip designs, such as many of the Log Cabin patterns, can be constructed directly on the batting and lining squares. In this instance, the seams of the strips should start and stop 1″ from the edges of the block. The two layers of fabric within this 1″ are then hand-sewn separately so that the batting and lining can be turned back to join the other blocks. Join the blocks in strips or sections and finish on the back by sewing the overlapped edges by hand.

Assembling Blocks by the Basic Quilt-As-You-Go Method

Quilt each block or section to within ½″ of the edges, then place two blocks together with the right sides touching *(Fig. 48)*. Trim the batting of the blocks so that the edges come just to the seamline *(Fig. 49)*. The edges of the batting should butt together when the blocks are opened out.

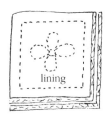

Fig. 48. *Place the blocks right sides together.*

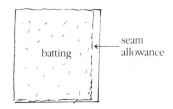

Fig. 49. *Trim the batting to the seamline.*

87

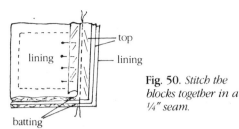

Fig. 50. *Stitch the blocks together in a ¼″ seam.*

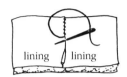

Fig. 51. *Blindstitch the edges of the lining together.*

Fold the lining layer on the top block out of the way and pin. Smooth out the top layer of each block and the lining of the bottom block and pin them together. Stitch the three layers together in a ¼″ seam *(Fig. 50)*. Turn the seam to one side, toward the lining of the top block.

Baste a ¼″ hem on the free edge of the lining. Lap this edge over the seam and blindstitch it in place *(Fig. 51)*.

Alternatively, you can stitch the blocks together through the top layer of fabric only. Turn under a ¼″ hem on one edge of the lining, lap it over the raw edge of the other block and blindstitch it in place.

When joining blocks in horizontal rows, turn all of the seams in odd-numbered rows in one direction; those in even-numbered rows should be turned in the opposite direction. When joining the rows, turn all of the seams in the same direction, either up or down.

Although the two designs that follow are very different in construction, and do not follow the basic method, both can be considered quilt-as-you-go techniques, since the quilt top, batting and lining are joined together section by section. Both designs are made entirely by machine, and are comforter-weight.

Enigma—A Hidden-Seam Comforter Made in Vertical Strips

Quilt Size: 68″ × 90″.

Materials for Quilt

Using the rotary cutter, cutting guide and mat, remove the selvages from the fabrics, then measure and cut the fabrics lengthwise as follows (all measurements include seam allowances)—

3 yds. vertical (lengthwise) floral striped fabric. Cut three strips 13″ wide by 92″ long for rows #2, 4 and 6.

3 yds. matching medium solid fabric. Cut four strips 6½″ wide by 92″ long for rows #1, 3, 5 and 7.

3 yds. matching dark solid fabric. Cut eight strips 1½″ wide by 92″ long for rows #1, 3, 5 and 7. Cut enough 2½″-wide bias strips from remaining fabric to make a strip long enough to go around all four sides of the quilt (10 yds.).

6 yds. lining fabric. Cut three strips 13″ wide by 92″ long, and four strips 8½″ wide by 92″ long. Cotton sateen makes a pretty lining. Two shades could be used to make the quilt reversible.

Queen-size quilt batt, ½″ thick. Cut three strips 13″ by 92″ and four strips 8½″ by 92″ for padding each strip.

This comforter-type quilt can easily be adjusted to any size, simply by adding more strips, or by making the strips wider or longer. The quilt shown in the diagram is for a standard double bed *(Fig. A)*.

Beautiful fabrics for this type of quilt can be found in the drapery fabrics section of your fabric store. Many lovely cotton sateens or other fabrics with a glazed finish are 50″–52″ wide, making them ideal for a king-size quilt. Choose a vertical floral pattern that can be cut into strips at least 13″ wide. Dress fabrics with wide, even vertical floral stripes can also be used.

In deciding the number of strips across the quilt, make sure the top design is balanced by beginning and ending the sides of the quilt with the same type of strip, either the wide printed floral or the pieced strips. Also, if the floral design has a widely spaced repeat pattern, plan to cut the fabric so that all of the strips begin at the same motif and match up across the quilt. First, lay out the floral fabric to determine how long your quilt will be and where to cut between the pattern repeats. Cut one floral strip, then cut the other floral strips by placing the first strip over the fabric and matching the pattern. The fabric for the pieced strips and the batting and lining strips will be cut this same length.

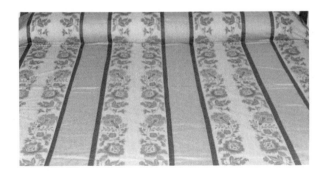

Fig. A. *The completed quilt.*

| Strip 1 | Strip 2 | Strip 3 | Strip 4 | Strip 5 | Strip 6 | Strip 7 |

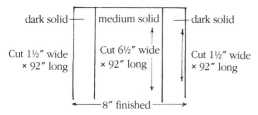

dark solid — medium solid — dark solid

Cut 1½" wide × 92" long — Cut 6½" wide × 92" long — Cut 1½" wide × 92" long

8" finished

Fig. B. *Sew a dark strip to each side of a medium strip.*

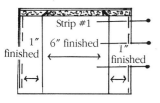

Strip #1

6" finished

1" finished — 1" finished

Fig. C. *Pin the layers together on the right; baste on the left.*

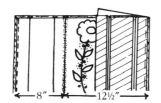

8" — 12½"

Fig. D. *Joining strip #3.*

Assembling the Quilt

Use ¼" seams throughout. Make pieced strips for rows #1, 3, 5 and 7 by sewing a dark solid strip to each edge of each medium solid strip (*Fig. B*).

You will now join the pieced and floral strips to form the quilt. Each strip is added to the right edge of the previous strip. Because of the thickness of the work, baste each seam before stitching.

Place the lining for strip #1, wrong side up, on the work surface; place the batting over it. Place pieced strip #1, right side up, on top of the batting. Pin the layers together on the right edge. Baste the left edge; this will be the left edge of the quilt (*Fig. C*).

Lay the #2 floral strip, wrong side up, on top of strip #1. Place the lining for strip #2, wrong side down, under strip #1 (the right side of the lining will be against strip #1). Pin, baste and stitch the layers together on the right edge. Place the quilt on the work surface as sewn, without turning the strips to the right side. Place the batting strip against the wrong side of strip #2 and baste it to the seam allowance only of the right edge. Turn strip #2 and its lining to the right side. The batting will be inside, attached to a hidden seam on the left edge. Pin the layers together on the right edge.

Place pieced strip #3, wrong side up, over strip #2. Place the lining, wrong side down, under strip #2 (*Fig. D*). Pin, baste and stitch the right-hand edge. The batting of strip #2 will be caught in the stitching. Place the quilt on the work surface and baste the batting to the seam allowance only. Turn the strips to the right side and pin the layers together on the right edge.

Continue to alternate the floral and pieced strips until all seven have been joined. Make sure that the floral strips are placed correctly so that the pattern repeats match up across the quilt. The quilt will begin and end with a pieced strip.

Trim the bottom edge of the quilt if necessary. Baste the edges of the quilt together. Bind the edges with the dark bias binding.

Spliced Channel Quilting

Quilt Size: 65" × 75".
Materials for Quilt
  45"-wide fabrics:
    1 yd. each of six harmonizing solid colors, some soft, some bright and some deep shades.
    4½ yds. for lining.
    2 full-size glazed quilt batts, ½" thick.

Although there appear to be thick rows of quilting across the work, this unusual technique actually involves no quilting at all. The strips are sewn to the lining layer, then padded with a folded strip of thick batting. All of the sewing is done by machine.

Make the lining first. Cut the lining fabric in half crosswise. From one piece, cut two strips 12" wide by the full length of the piece. Sew a narrow strip to each long edge of the uncut length. Press the seams open. Trim the lining to measure 65" × 75". Place the lining, wrong side up, on the work surface. Measuring very carefully, mark a line across the lining 1½" from the top edge. Mark additional lines across the lining 1½" apart. These will be used as guidelines for attaching the strips.

Spliced Channel Quilting

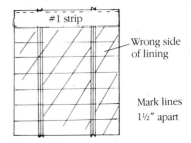

Fig. A. *Top-stitch the first strip to the wrong side of the lining.*

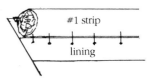

Fig. B. *Pin the fabric strip over the roll of batting.*

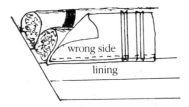

Fig. C. *Sew on additional strips.*

Fig. D. *The completed quilt.*

Cutting across the full width of the fabric, cut the colored fabrics into 3″-wide strips with the rotary cutter. Cut the strips into shorter lengths, then join the shorter lengths end to end, varying the colors, to form 65″-long strips. This "splicing" can be done at random, or you can work out a color plan on graph paper before beginning. If you work with a specific color plan, be sure to add seam allowances to the ends of the strips before cutting them.

Pin the first long strip, right side up, across the wrong side of the lining, with the raw edges matching. Top-stitch ¼″ from the edge *(Fig. A)*.

Cut a 6″ by 65″ strip of batting. Fold it lengthwise into thirds to make a 2″-wide roll. Lift up the fabric strip and place the rolled batting against the seam. Roll the fabric strip over the batting and match the raw edge to the first line marked on the lining. Pin the edge in many places *(Fig. B)*.

Place the second long fabric strip, wrong side up, across the lining over the first strip, with the raw edges matching. Stitch across ¼″ from the raw edges through both strips and the lining *(Fig. C)*. Place a roll of batting against the seam; roll the fabric strip over the batting, matching the raw edge of the strip to the next line on the lining, and pin securely.

Continue adding strips and padding until the lining is covered *(Fig. D)*. Attach the edge of the last strip to the lining by top stitching ¼″ from the bottom edge.

Before binding the edges of the quilt, remove about ½″ of stuffing from each end of each roll. Pin a tiny tuck in the top layer to flatten the end against the lining. Baste the side edges to hold the tucks in place. Cut 2½″-wide bias binding and bind the edge of the quilt.

To make a padded binding, cut strips for the sides 4″ wide by the length of the quilt, cutting on the straight grain of the fabric. With the right sides together, pin a strip to one side of the quilt and stitch. Place a roll of batting against the seam; roll the strip over the batting to the back side. Turn in the raw edge of the strip and blindstitch it to the lining. Repeat on the other side.

Cut the strips for the ends, 4″ wide and 6″ longer than the width of the quilt. Fold in a 3″ hem on each end and attach the strips to the quilt as for the sides. Catch-stitch the hems on each end.